GREAT MYSTERIES

Alien Abductions

OPPOSING VIEWPOINTS®

Look for these and other exciting *Great Mysteries: Opposing Viewpoints* books:

GREAT MYSTERIES

Alien Abductions

OPPOSING VIEWPOINTS®

by Patricia D. Netzley

Greenhaven Press, Inc.   P.O. Box 289009, San Diego, California 92198-9009

Library of Congress Cataloging-in-Publication Data

Netzley, Patricia D.
    Alien abductions : opposing viewpoints / by Patricia D. Netzley.
        p.   cm. — (Great mysteries)
    Includes bibliographical references and index.
    ISBN 1-56510-352-1
    1. Unidentified flying objects—Sightings and encounters.
    2. Abduction.   I. Title.   II. Series: Great mysteries (Saint Paul,
    Minn.)
    TL789.3.N48   1996
    001.9'42—dc20   95-25106
                                                                    CIP

© 1996 by Greenhaven Press, Inc.
Printed in the U.S.A.

To Ray, Matthew, Sarah, and Jacob for their love,
to Brenda Ulyate, Cynthia Lewis, and Eleanor Morgan for their friendship,
and to the Fabers for their support.

Contents

Introduction

This book is written for the curious—those who want to explore the mysteries that are everywhere. To be human is to be constantly surrounded by wonderment. How do birds fly? Are ghosts real? Can animals and people communicate? Was King Arthur a real person or a myth? Why did Amelia Earhart disappear? Did history really happen the way we think it did? Where did the world come from? Where is it going?

Great Mysteries: Opposing Viewpoints books are intended to offer the reader an opportunity to explore some of the many mysteries that both trouble and intrigue us. For the span of each book, we want the reader to feel that he or she is a scientist investigating the extinction of the dinosaurs, an archaeologist searching for clues to the origin of the great Egyptian pyramids, a psychic detective testing the existence of ESP.

One thing all mysteries have in common is that there is no ready answer. Often there are *many* answers but none on which even the majority of authorities agrees. *Great Mysteries: Opposing Viewpoints* books introduce the intriguing views of the experts, allowing the reader to participate in their explorations, their theories, and their disagreements as they try to explain the mysteries of our world.

But most readers won't want to stop here. These *Great Mysteries: Opposing Viewpoints* aim to stimulate the reader's curiosity. Although truth is often impossible to discover, the search is fascinating. It is up to the reader to examine the evidence, to decide whether the answer is there—or to explore further.

"Penetrating so many secrets, we cease to believe in the unknowable. But there it sits nevertheless, calmly licking its chops."

H.L. Mencken, American essayist

Prologue

From Sightings to Kidnappings

(Opposite page) Three domed-shaped objects that appear to be mysterious flying craft hover over the Italian countryside in this 1960 photo. The question of whether aliens exist has baffled and intrigued humans since ancient times.

Unidentified flying objects, or UFOs, first appeared in ancient times. Since then, thousands of people have reported seeing them. Many scientists believe these UFOs are optical illusions, but witnesses say the objects must be spacecraft from another planet.

Astronomers argue that reports of visitors from other planets must be false. Astronomers have scanned the galaxies for years and never detected any intelligent life on other planets. They believe that aliens would certainly try to contact us before coming to earth. In the book *UFO's—A Scientific Debate*, astronomer Carl Sagan explains:

> I believe . . . UFOs as interstellar vehicles is extremely unlikely. . . . One may argue that space flight is not the most cost-effective way to communicate between civilizations and that interstellar radio contact is a better way. . . . We do not know enough to exclude such visitations, but the probability of such visitations seems very small.

Close Encounters of the Fourth Kind

Sagan assumes that aliens do not exist because scientists have not seen them or received messages from them. But what if these creatures have a

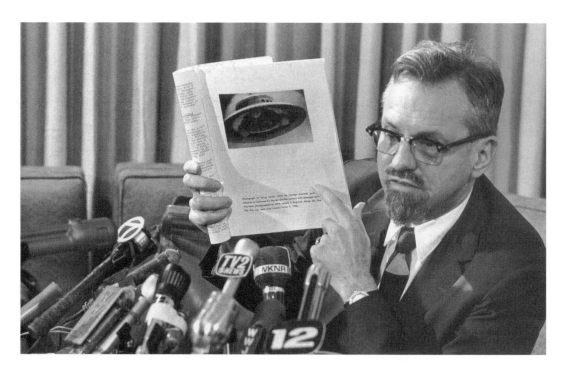

J. Allen Hynek, shown holding a photo of an alleged alien spacecraft, developed a classification system that organized alien contact into five categories. According to Hynek's system, an alien abduction is classified as a "close encounter of the fourth kind."

reason to hide themselves? What if they are visiting earth for a purpose they want to keep secret?

This is the belief of people who claim not only to have *seen* a UFO but also to have been *abducted* by one. These "abductees" say UFOs are spaceships piloted by aliens who kidnap humans, examine them, and then let them go. Abductees suggest that their alien kidnappers might not want earth's scientists to know about them.

When abductees first started saying these things, they were not taken seriously. Then UFO researchers, or ufologists, decided to study alien abduction. They labeled this kind of alien contact a "close encounter of the fourth kind," following a method of UFO classification developed by ufologist J. Allen Hynek.

According to Hynek's system, a close encounter of the first kind is when someone merely sees a UFO. A close encounter of the second kind is when the UFO affects the environment around it in some way—for example, by leaving a burn mark on the ground. A close encounter of the third kind is when someone sees aliens around a UFO. A close encounter of the fourth kind is when someone is abducted by aliens. A close encounter of the fifth kind is when someone has extensive mental contact with aliens who send messages telepathically, using voices and images.

Very few individuals have reported a close encounter of the fifth kind, but thousands have reported first-kind experiences. The number of those who have experienced a close encounter of the fourth kind is in great dispute.

Some ufologists believe that less than a thousand people can accurately be called abductees. Other investigators argue that the number is far higher, and even suggest that many abductees might as yet be unidentified. Perhaps abductees might be afraid to come forward or, because of blocked memories, might not even know they had been abducted.

Differing Opinions

Four researchers have conducted more abductee interviews than perhaps anyone else. Ufologists Budd Hopkins and David Jacobs have evaluated several hundred abduction cases. Harvard psychiatrist John Mack interviewed about a hundred abductees. University of Connecticut psychologist Kenneth Ring examined ninety-seven people who reported a wide range of UFO encounters, including abduction, for a research study called the Omega Project. These men all believe that abductees have had a valid experience.

Ufologist Raymond Fowler has also investigated the abduction phenomenon. His research has led him to conclude that alien abductions exist in a physical reality. In other words, aliens are not an

Based on his investigation of hundreds of abduction cases, ufologist Budd Hopkins concluded that alien abductions are a physical reality.

"Is it conceivable that all of the UFO reports can be due to mistakes and hoaxes? I think that it is conceivable, and not at all a rash suggestion."

William K. Hartman, professor of planetary science, in *UFO's—A Scientific Debate*

"You'll find it . . . tough to tell tens of thousands of people that UFOs and the beings associated with them are delusions or hoaxes. Too many observers have seen too many things to simply dismiss all sightings out of hand. To claim the data is all false is to call into question consensus reality itself. If that many reports can be wrong by that degree, any observation by humans isn't worth the brain it's processed by."

Bufo Calvin, in *Strange* magazine

illusion. In his book *The Watchers: The Secret Design Behind UFO Abduction*, Fowler says:

> Reports exist from credible, sane persons who claim to have been abducted by creatures described by nonabductee witnesses. Many elements within their abduction accounts have a commonality. . . . In some cases similar physical marks are left on the abductees' bodies. All of these elements provide strong circumstantial evidence that abductions are grounded in reality.

Abductees offer their own opinions about what has happened to them. Some believe they have had a real experience. Others suggest alternate explanations for the abduction phenomenon.

Bizarro by Dan Piraro is reprinted by permission of Chronicle Features, San Francisco, California.

For example, abductee Whitley Strieber believes that human beings might be causing their own abductions. Perhaps something in earth's gravity or the planet's electromagnetic fields produces abduction images in the brain. In Kenneth Ring's book *The Omega Project: Near-Death Experiences, UFO Encounters, and Mind at Large*, Strieber says:

> I strongly suspect that the experience represents a response to some natural phenomenon, probably of an electromagnetic nature. . . . I say this because . . . I have been able to observe details of its intelligence that so strongly point to its human origins that I can only say that, if aliens are here, they have learned to mimic the inner mind of man.

Meanwhile, UFO disbelievers, or skeptics, argue that all abductees have to be lying, fantasizing, dreaming, or hallucinating. For example, well-known skeptic Philip Klass says he is certain no one will ever prove that UFOs are real. In his book *UFO Abductions*, Klass writes:

> After having spent more than 22 years investigating famous, seemingly mysterious UFO reports—including some of the earliest claims of UFO abduction—I can assure you that there is absolutely no scientifically credible physical evidence to indicate that the earth is being visited by extraterrestrials—let alone that they are abducting people.

What are we to believe? What causes the abduction experience? Are aliens really visiting earth and experimenting on people, or is there a more mundane explanation for this mystery? These questions have prompted much passionate debate.

One

Suspecting Abduction: The Hill Case

On the night of September 19, 1961, Betty and Barney Hill were driving along a deserted road from Canada to their home in Portsmouth, New Hampshire. The sky was full of stars. Suddenly, Betty noticed a strange light moving rapidly among the stars.

She and her husband stopped their car several times to study the object through binoculars. It kept changing direction and appeared to have lights on only one side. As it spun around, the lights seemed to wink on and off.

Betty became excited. She knew she was seeing a UFO! But Barney disagreed. He insisted the lights had to be coming from an airplane. Then the object came closer.

In a letter to Major Donald Keyhoe, founder of the National Investigations Committee on Aerial Phenomena (NICAP), Betty describes what happened next:

(Opposite page) Betty Hill looks on as her husband Barney points to a sketch of the spacecraft they say abducted them as they drove along a deserted New Hampshire road in 1961. The Hills' highly publicized case started a rash of similar reports.

As it approached our car, we stopped again. As it hovered in the air in front of us, it appeared to be pancake in shape, ringed with windows in the front through which we could see bright blue-white lights. Suddenly, two red lights appeared on each side. By this time my husband was

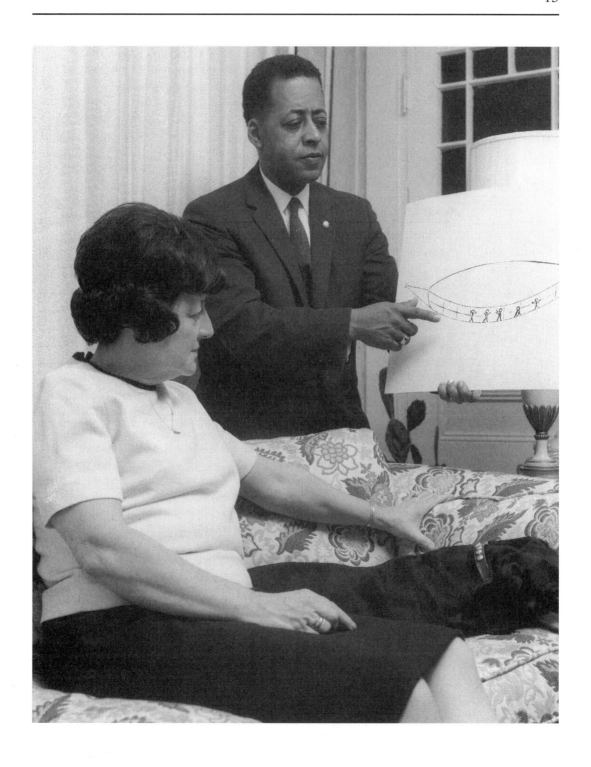

standing in the road, watching closely [through binoculars]. He saw wings protrude on each side and the red lights were on the wing tips.

As it glided closer he was able to see inside this object, but not too closely. He did see several figures scurrying about as though they were making some hurried type of preparation. One figure was observing us from the windows. From the distance this was seen, the figures appeared to be about the size of a pencil [held at arm's length], and seemed to be dressed in some type of shiny black uniform.

Barney jumped back into the car, and the Hills sped away. Suddenly they began to feel drowsy. When their alertness returned, they were still driving—but their car was thirty-five miles farther down the road and the time was two hours later.

Missing Time

This kind of missing time is often the first clue that an abduction experience has taken place. David Jacobs, in his book *Secret Life: Firsthand Documented Accounts of UFO Abductions*, explains:

Missing-time episodes are common in abductees' lives. They are unable to account for a "lost" period of time, which might be as short as an hour or two or as long as a day—and sometimes even longer. Trying to understand the origin of the missing time can torture the victims. It makes no sense. They have no explanation, and yet they know it happened.

When Betty and Barney Hill returned home after their UFO encounter, they did not remember anything other than seeing an alien spacecraft in the sky. However, ten days after seeing the UFO, Betty began to have disturbing nightmares. She dreamed that she and Barney were aboard a strange spacecraft, where alien beings examined them. The aliens told Betty that when they were finished with her, she would have no conscious memory of her experience.

At the same time, Barney also began showing signs of trauma. He had symptoms of emotional distress. He suffered panic attacks and developed an ulcer. Finally he decided to seek psychiatric help to discover the cause of his condition.

In 1964, three years after sighting the UFO, the Hills decided to undergo hypnosis. Hypnosis is a therapist-induced mental state that can help people remember forgotten events. A person under hypnosis answers a series of questions designed to elicit important information. Under hypnosis the Hills remembered that aliens had indeed taken them aboard their spaceship, put them in separate rooms, and physically examined them before letting them go.

The Hills became convinced that they had spent those missing two hours aboard an alien spacecraft. However, Philip Klass has a more ordinary explanation for the Hills' missing time. He does not believe anything unusual happened during those two hours. Instead he thinks the Hills simply failed to keep track of their time. In his book *UFO Abductions* Klass says:

> If a UFO was indeed following them as they drove along Highway 3, as both . . . suspected, it would be logical to divert to a less conspicuous road. (Later, Betty would recall that they had turned off onto Highway 175, and later onto an obscure side road. Perhaps they had even pulled off the road in the hope they could shake the UFO.)
>
> Considering these diversions and time spent later trying to find their way back to the main highway, it is not surprising that they arrived back in Portsmouth roughly two hours later than originally expected.

Postabduction Syndrome

Betty's dreams and Barney's distress were part of what many psychologists now call postabduction syndrome. Postabduction syndrome (PAS) is a

Under hypnosis Barney Hill remembered that he and Betty had been abducted by aliens during the two hours for which they were unable to account.

specific collection of psychological symptoms that appear in people who claim to have been abducted by aliens. PAS can be mild or severe, depending on the individual abductee.

Like Barney, PAS sufferers often experience anxiety, depression, or both. They become extremely upset over small problems. They might also have irrational fears. Most PAS sufferers are afraid to be alone, and many are afraid of roads or fields. David Jacobs says:

> They may have traveled the same route for years without giving it a thought, but one day they become inordinately afraid of it. They stop traveling on that stretch of road, and go miles out of their way to avoid it. Child abductees who have played in a nearby park every day suddenly are afraid to go there and never want to play there again. They may have suffered strange missing-time episodes at these places, and they will agonize over what happened to them for many years.

Nightmares

PAS sufferers usually have trouble sleeping. They are afraid to go to bed, and many leave lights or radios on for comfort. As with Betty Hill, if they do manage to sleep, they wake frequently and often have vivid nightmares about strange alien beings.

These dreams sometimes intrude on daily activities. For example, abductee Debbie Jordan found herself reliving her dreams during the day. In the book *Abducted!* she explains:

> My nightmares had begun to seep into my waking state and I had begun to have what I called flashbacks. I could be involved in the most mundane task with my mind blank and suddenly start to see whole scenes whiz before my eyes as if I were watching them on a movie screen. And I was the unwilling star. Sometimes I would only see eyes. These huge, liquid black eyes, boring a

hole through me. At other times I would see whole faces, gray faces with slits for mouths.

Mysterious Events

Besides PAS, abductees have other things in common. When Betty and Barney Hill regained awareness after their experience, they found themselves miles away from where they should have been. David Jacobs says that many people "come to consciousness . . . miles away from where they should have been—not just down the road but on a completely different highway."

Abductees taken from home can also regain awareness in a place other than the one in which their experience began. For example, Patti Layne fell asleep in her room and woke up on her bathroom floor. Debbie Jordan found herself outside. Often an abductee gets out of bed in the morning to discover unexplained grass, leaves, or twigs on his or her clothes or feet. Jacobs reports:

> Many abductees have returned to find oddities about their clothes and bodies. It is not unusual for people to notice that their pajamas or nightgowns are on inside out when they felt certain that they had put them on the correct way the night before. . . . Some abductees have reported that their clothes were draped around a chair when they woke up in the morning.

Other abductees discover strange scars on their bodies. Raymond Fowler, in his book *The Watchers*, describes his shock at finding such a mark on himself while taking a shower:

> I stared at the side of my lower leg in astonishment. A disquieting aura of disbelief and denial crept over my transfixed wet body. There, just as plain as could be, was a freshly cut scoop mark. I shut off the shower and felt the perfectly round indentation. There was no pain and no signs of bleeding. It looked like a miniature cookie cutter had removed a perfectly round piece of flesh.

The Hills decided to share their story with others. In 1965 an article about their abduction appeared in a Boston newspaper. The following year author John G. Fuller published an entire book about their case, entitled *The Interrupted Journey: Two Lost Hours "Aboard a Flying Saucer."* When *Look* magazine wrote about *The Interrupted Journey* in October 1966, the Hills became famous.

Fuller's book reproduced partial transcripts of the statements the Hills made while under hypnosis. Each one's memories of what happened during their missing time were basically the same, although Betty offered far more details.

Her abduction experience began when she and Barney saw a group of strange-looking men standing in the middle of the road. Barney stopped the car and its engine immediately died, whereupon the aliens removed the couple from the car. *The Interrupted Journey* quotes Betty's recollection:

The Hills hold a copy of *The Interrupted Journey*, which chronicles their alleged abduction experience. The book, filled with statements made by the Hills under hypnosis, made the couple famous.

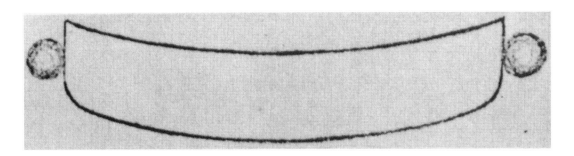

I'm thinking I'm asleep . . . I'm asleep, and I've got to wake up. . . . But even though I'm asleep, I'm walking! And there's . . . a couple of men behind me, and then there's Barney. There's a man on each side of him. And my eyes are open . . . but Barney's still asleep. He's walking, and he's asleep. . . . And I turn around, and I say, "Barney! Wake up! *Barney!* Why don't you wake up?" And he doesn't pay any attention. He keeps walking. . . . And then the man walking beside me here says, "Oh, is his name Barney?" . . . And I wouldn't answer him, so he says . . . "Don't be afraid. You don't have any reason to be afraid. We're not going to harm you, but we just want to do some tests. When the tests are over with, we'll take you and Barney back and put you in your car. You'll be on your way back home in no time."

Betty Hill's sketch of the alien spaceship that she claims kidnapped her and her husband.

Betty's Physical Examination

Betty then recalled walking up a ramp into a spaceship, where the aliens put Barney in one room and her in another. Betty's next memories were of a physical examination:

And the examiner opens my eyes, and looks in them with a light and he opens my mouth, and he looks in my throat and [at] my teeth and he looks in my ears, and he turned my head, and he looked in this ear. . . . And then the doctor, the examiner says he wants to do some tests, he wants to check my nervous system. And I am thinking, I don't know how our nervous systems

"Surreptitious examinations such as those conducted on Betty and Barney Hill made a great deal of sense, especially when contrasted with the foolish 'landing-on-the-White-House-lawn-take-us-to-your-leader' concept of what we should expect."

Budd Hopkins, *Missing Time*

"Now the abductionists are actually claiming a . . . figure of *nine million abductions for the United States alone*, in support of their theory that UFOs are extraterrestrial spacecraft. This would translate to nearly two hundred million abductees for the whole planet. Such statistics actually prove the opposite of what they try to prove. The aliens would have to be very poor scientists indeed if they needed that many interventions to collect the kind of material any skilled human nurse could collect in a few hours, and without inducing trauma."

Jacques Vallee, *Revelations*

are, but I hope we never have nerve enough to go around kidnapping people right off the highways, as he has done!

Betty remembered that the aliens used a strange device to touch her on various parts of her head. Although this part of the examination wasn't painful, other parts were. Betty says:

So then . . . the examiner has a long needle in his hand . . . and it's bigger than any needle that I've ever seen. And I ask him what he's going to do with it . . . and he said he just wants to put it in my navel, it's just a simple test. And I tell him no, it will hurt, don't do it, don't do it. And I'm crying, and I'm telling him, "It's hurting, it's hurting, take it out, take it out!" And the leader comes over and he puts his hand, rubs his hand in front of my eyes, and he says it will be all right. I won't feel it. And all the pain goes away. The pain goes away, but I'm still sore from where they put that needle. I don't know why they put that needle into my navel. Because I told them they shouldn't do it.

Betty Answers Questions

According to Betty, when the aliens finished examining her, they showed her a star map. They asked her if she knew where earth was on the map, but she had no idea. They asked her more questions and sometimes seemed confused about her answers. For example, they wanted to know what human beings ate but did not understand the word *vegetables*.

They also puzzled over differences between her and Barney. Betty remembers:

The examiner said that they could not figure it out—Barney's teeth came out, and mine didn't. I was really laughing, and said Barney had dentures, and I didn't, and that is why his teeth came out. So then they asked me, "What are dentures?" And I said people as they got older lost their teeth. They had to go to a dentist and have their teeth extracted, and they put in dentures. . . . And the leader said, "Well, does this happen to many people?" He . . . acted as if he didn't believe me.

Barney's Memories

Barney's memories under hypnosis were not as complete as Betty's memories. Some parts of his abduction experience were missing. Still, he recalled being examined. He says: "I was very afraid to open my eyes. I had been told not to open my eyes, and it would be over with quickly. And I could feel them examining me with their hands." At the end of the abduction, Barney remembers:

> And I think I felt very good because I knew it was over. And again, I was led to the door . . . and [I] went back toward the ramp. And I went down and opened my eyes and kept walking. And I saw my car, and the lights were out. And it was sitting down the road and very dark. And I couldn't understand. I had not turned off the lights. . . . And Betty was coming down the road, and she came around and opened the door.

A Basis for Disbelief

When Dr. Benjamin Simon, the Boston psychiatrist who hypnotized the Hills, heard their full story, he dismissed it as untrue. Dr. Simon could not accept that aliens might exist. Therefore, he decided that the Hills' experience had to be some kind of dream or fantasy. In *The Interrupted Journey*, Dr.

Barney Hill drew what he saw through his binoculars before he and Betty were abducted. The sketch shows the lights on each side of the spacecraft and aliens peering from the windows.

> "If we had expected to encounter any kind of living beings, which, of course, we didn't, we would naturally have asked NASA to put us down in some very unpopulated region where we could examine the local fauna in safety and at our discretion. We would have wanted to pick up some living specimens, examine them, and put them back with a minimum of fuss, hoping to get back to earth safely with as much information as possible."
>
> Dr. Edgar Mitchell, astronaut who walked on the moon during the second landing, in *Missing Time*

> "The public is subtly being taught that UFOs, if they exist, are necessarily extraterrestrial vehicles and cannot be anything else. Here the ufologists are actually resorting to the worst argument of their old skeptical adversaries, namely ridicule, to purge the dissenters from their ranks. Yet some of the major scientific figures who have carefully researched the data . . . concurred as early as the mid-seventies that the extraterrestrial theory was unsatisfactory."
>
> Jacques Vallee, *Revelations*

Simon says: "Anything beyond that would seem to stretch the limits of credulity too far."

Different Memories

Dr. Simon based his conclusion in part on the fact that Betty recalled parts of the experience that Barney did not. To Dr. Simon this meant that they could not both have gone through the same event. As Philip Klass, in his book *UFO Abduction*s, explains:

> Under regressive hypnosis, which was used as a memory aid, Betty recalled many details of the alleged abduction while Barney could recall very few. This, Dr. Simon emphasized, showed that the alleged abduction was *not* a shared experience. The psychiatrist was at first puzzled over how Barney had acquired even a few details of the incident. But he learned that Betty enjoyed recounting her abduction dreams to friends, neighbors, and UFO investigators and that Barney often was present on those occasions, sometimes reading the newspaper or watching television.

Dr. Simon did believe that the Hills had sighted a UFO in the sky, but he suspected that the source of their abduction story was Betty's dreams. He felt that many things Betty said did not make sense, a frequent characteristic of dreams. Klass explains:

> [Dr. Simon] found that the tale [Betty] told under regressive hypnosis was essentially identical to her nightmare dreams. When I asked Dr. Simon how he could be sure that the original nightmares were not themselves based on an actual experience, he pointed out a few of the many irrational inconsistencies of the abduction story. He stressed that such inconsistencies are characteristic of dreams.
>
> For example . . . the ETs [extraterrestrials] were familiar enough with earthly gadgets to know how to operate the zipper on her dress. But they were completely baffled by the fact that

After listening to a tape recording of himself under hypnosis, Barney Hill drew this sketch of one of his abductors.

Barney's teeth could be removed, while Betty's were firmly anchored. Betty said she tried to explain to one of the spacemen that when some people get older they need artificial teeth, but he could not comprehend what was meant by age or the passage of time. Yet later, Betty said, when she was about to leave the flying saucer, the same spaceman said to her, "Wait a minute."

Credible Witnesses

But those who knew the Hills felt that these inconsistencies were unimportant or could be explained. They pointed out that both Betty and Barney were respected, church-going members of their community and active in local and national politics. The Hills were highly credible witnesses.

As a result, many people decided the couple was telling the truth. For example, Budd Hopkins was an artist and sculptor when he first read about the Hills. Their story led him to become a ufologist. In his book *Missing Time*, Hopkins says:

As I read about the case in detail—[in] Fuller's book, *The Interrupted Journey*—I began to feel

This sketch by Barney Hill, drawn four years after the abduction incident, was made from his recollections of the inside of the spaceship.

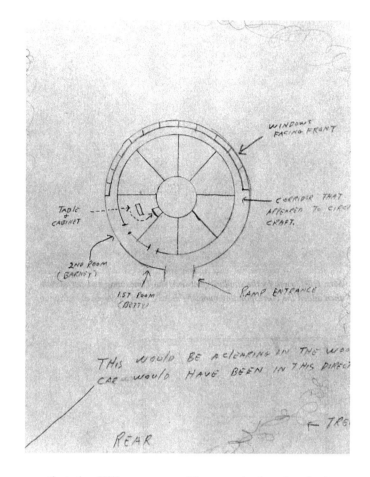

that the Hills were recalling precisely what had happened to them, and the fact that it emerged the way it did, under hypnosis, in two separate accounts, gave it unusual validity. If the UFOs were some kind of spacecraft piloted—if that's the word—by extraterrestrials, perhaps they might be exploring very cautiously, giving us a good long look, picking up "samples" under very safe conditions, really studying us at long range before landing and establishing contact.

More Abduction Stories Surface

Once the Hills' story became well known, other people said they too had been abducted by aliens.

Their abduction stories were remarkably similar to the Hills' story. The same details appeared in many of the accounts, which led more and more ufologists to suspect that abductions were real.

As the number of abductee reports increased, psychiatrists began in-depth studies of the phenomenon. They developed certain guidelines for evaluating abduction stories and formed certain conclusions about what might be happening to abductees. Meanwhile, skeptics focused on what was wrong with abduction research, continued to point out problems with the Hill case, and attacked all subsequent abduction claims.

Two

After the Hills: Evaluating Abduction Stories

(Opposite page) Physicist and UFO lecturer Stanton Friedman holds a photo of a sculpture of an alien, created by a New Hampshire man who claims to have been abducted in 1971. Determining how to evaluate the validity of abduction stories has put skeptics and believers at odds.

Only one other abduction story had been published prior to the Hill case. It was a 1965 account concerning Antonio Villas-Boas from Brazil. Villas-Boas claimed that several years earlier he had seen a spaceship land and been given a bizarre physical examination by its alien crew. Ufologists dismissed this account as unbelievable, and most people never heard about it.

After the Hill case, however, more people began to tell abduction stories. When two men in Pascagoula, Mississippi, reported being abducted and examined in 1973, the media took the story seriously. The same was true when woodcutter Travis Walton reported an abduction experience in 1975. By the 1990s, hundreds of people were calling themselves abductees.

Deliberate Liars

Skeptic Philip Klass believes the Hill case *caused* all these other abduction reports. He thinks that people who claim to be abductees are simply seeking attention. Klass believes others made up their stories after reading Fuller's book *The Interrupted Journey* or watching a 1975 TV movie about the Hills. However, he has no proof to back up his claim.

UFO investigator Joseph Santangelo listens as Betty Andreasson relives her abduction ordeal through hypnosis.

Ufologists say that their research indicates few abductees have been influenced by books or movies about alien abduction. They admit that a few abductees have indeed made up their stories, but say that most abductees are people of good character with no apparent reason to lie. A majority of abductees avoid publicity and do not profit from their experiences.

In addition, approximately 70 percent first remember their abduction experience during the process of hypnosis. Many ufologists say this means abductees cannot be lying, because hypnosis uncovers memories of true experiences only.

But Klass argues that hypnotism does not always lead to the truth. He says people under hypnosis are just as capable of lying as people not under hypnosis. In *UFO Abductions*, Klass quotes Dr. Martin T. Orne, a professor of psychiatry and leading expert on hypnosis: "It is possible for even deeply hypnotized subjects to willfully lie [and for] an individual to feign hypnosis and deceive even highly experienced hypnotists."

Ufologist Raymond Fowler agrees with Klass that people can and do lie while under hypnosis. But he believes that hypnotism cannot suddenly turn an honest person into a dishonest one. In *The Watchers*

Fowler says: "An honest person seeking only the truth would not willfully lie under hypnosis."

Fowler believes that certain psychological traits indicate whether a person is inherently truthful or prone to lying and says that psychologists can test for these traits. He concludes that "the accuracy of memories hypnotically retrieved by a skilled hypnotist is directly related to the psychological makeup of the subject."

False Memories

Fowler's arguments concern honesty and dishonesty. He is discussing whether abductees under hypnosis are intentionally lying about being abducted. But what if they are lying *unintentionally?*

The human mind can be highly unreliable. People sometimes misremember actual events, distorting some of the details of what happened, or recall things that never really occurred. In both instances, they are not intentionally lying.

Two researchers, Dr. Elizabeth Loftus and Katherine Ketcham, have studied both kinds of false memories. In their book *The Myth of Repressed Memory*, they explain that such inaccuracies come from our desire to create explanations. Loftus and Ketcham say:

> Our memories tell us stories, and we listen, enthralled. We want to know what happened in our past, we need our questions answered, we seek to resolve our uncertainty and ambiguity. Memory, our most loyal and faithful servant, complies with our wishes.

In other words, the mind of someone who has unexplained scars might create a story to explain those scars: perhaps the injuries did happen on a spaceship during experiments conducted by aliens. This false memory might seem perfectly real. It might also be enhanced by hypnosis.

Some ufologists argue that abductions cannot be false memories because of their many details—how could hypnotized people create such complex stories? But psychologists have much evidence that the human mind can create details where none exist. Philip Klass cites one study in which people remembering their childhoods under hypnosis "would describe their classmates so vividly and with such conviction that we were surprised indeed to find, when we went to the trouble of checking the actual school records, that some of these individuals had not been members of the subject's class."

Loftus and Ketcham tell of another study in which a staged robbery was committed. Afterwards the victims and witnesses viewed a movie that contained false details about the crime. Later they were asked to remember what happened. Researchers discovered that a majority had incorporated the false details into their versions of what happened.

More significantly, the witnesses said they were absolutely certain their memories were correct. Loftus and Ketcham state: "Subjects typically resisted any suggestion that their richly detailed memories might have been flawed or contaminated and asserted with great confidence that they saw what their revised and adapted memories told them they saw." In other words, these people were as insistent as abductees were about the accuracy of their stories.

Uncertain Memories

Such research suggests that all memories are highly suspect. Even when people are "certain" of a particular truth, they can be wrong. The human mind is easily influenced by movies and stories about an event.

Hypnosis makes the mind even easier to influence. Hypnotists therefore must be careful about the way they phrase their questions. For example, asking abductees, "How did you get your scar?" is very different from asking them, "Do you think your scar might have come from some kind of strange medical procedure?"

UFO skeptic Philip Klass says poor questioning is the reason ufologist Budd Hopkins has uncovered so many cases of alien abduction. He believes Hopkins subtly encourages his hypnotized subjects to tell detailed abduction stories. According to Klass, Hopkins's abductees are very eager for his approval and will say anything while under hypnosis to please him.

A Refusal to Be Led

In contrast, David Jacobs does not believe a hypnotist can make a person create an abduction experience. In his book *Secret Life*, Jacobs says that "experience has shown that most abductees refuse to be led" during their hypnosis. He offers Betty and Barney Hill as examples. He explains that although the Hills' therapist, Dr. Simon, tried many times to get them to accept their abduction story as merely a dream, they would not. Jacobs concludes:

> The investigators, hypnotists, and researchers have learned about abductions not by imposing some sort of purposeful structure on abductee accounts but by patiently listening to what the abductees say. Furthermore, a significant percentage of abduction accounts are related by the abductee without the aid of hypnosis. Their stories are essentially the same as those related while under hypnosis.

Jacobs finds this fact important. If unhypnotized people are remembering the same details as hypnotized ones, then no one can say these details are coming from the subtle hints of a hypnotist.

Common Elements

Many researchers have confirmed that abductees tell similar stories whether or not they are under hypnosis. These stories follow a common sequence of events. Abductee descriptions of the aliens, their ships, and their examination procedures remain fairly constant.

"NBC-TV's prime-time movie 'The UFO Incident' [about Betty and Barney Hill] . . . provided useful details for those who later would claim that they too had been abducted."

Philip Klass, *UFO Abductions*

"Abductee claims contain events that include exact and minute details of procedures known only to a few UFO researchers. It is virtually impossible that nearly all abductees would chance upon these details at random and lie en masse to make their claims seem valid. . . . Most abductees do not know each other, do not know much about UFOs, and are not familiar with abduction literature."

David Jacobs, *Secret Life*

Alan Godfrey, who claims to have been abducted by aliens in England in 1980, sketches pictures of his abductors.

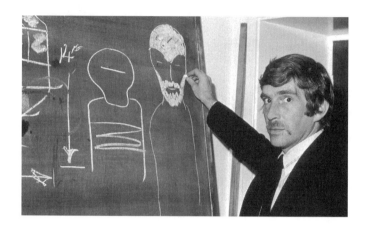

All abductees report being taken from an isolated location, whether it is a deserted road, a forest, or a private home. Jacobs says: "Secrecy appears to be critically important to the aliens in determining the opportunities for abductions. . . . No abductions have surfaced that took place in the middle of a very large group of people, in full view at a public event."

Some abductees went to these secluded places by choice, but others insist they were drawn to them by a sudden, inexplicable urge. In *The Omega Project* by Kenneth Ring, one abductee says:

> I was driving from Columbus to Marion when I felt compelled to turn into a state park area. I drove into the park about a mile, stopped the car and got out. A bright light was hovering high in the sky over the trees. I stood beside the car and stared at the light. It descended into the trees in front of me. I walked through the trees to the UFO which was sitting on the ground *not* glowing. I went into the UFO.

Most abductees are alone when their experience begins, but a few are part of a small group. In these cases, they report that the aliens chose to abduct only one or two people from the group, leaving the rest behind in some kind of trance. The trance ends when the abductees return.

Jacobs illustrates this point with the story of Will Parker. Parker and his wife, Ginny, were driving through Virginia late at night. Suddenly, Parker had the urge to pull into a closed gas station and turn off his engine. The couple heard a noise, and Parker saw an alien approach. Under hypnosis, he reported:

> [I see a] little guy, he's outside the car, and he's not human. He's, he ought to be cold because he hasn't got a coat on. . . . Now Ginny is quiet. I'm turning to her, but she's just, she's asleep is what she is. . . . I'm scared for Ginny because I don't know how she's going to, she's not going to remember. . . . [The aliens] told me she's not going to remember.

Ginny remained "asleep" until Parker returned.

Like Parker, most abductees leave quietly with their aliens, whom they say have placed them in another kind of trance. However, some people report a more traumatic experience. Abductee David Masters tells Kenneth Ring:

> Three "people" got out of the small craft. Two of these guys were 4 to 5 feet tall and grey-colored. The other one was brown-colored and much larger than the other two. . . . I began to run. The big brown guy was on me in a flash, forcing me back to the small craft. I resisted and was shocked repeatedly with an "electric" sort of gadget. I continued to resist. They shocked me into unconsciousness. They did so brutally, viciously. I came to and allowed myself to be forced into the small craft.

Aliens in the House

Abductees taken from private homes report similar experiences. They say that aliens entered their rooms on beams of light, usually through windows—open or closed. These aliens either examined people within the house or took them to their spaceship first by walking them, carrying them, or floating them away.

Greta Lincoln's abduction experience is typical. She tells Ring:

> I was 5 years old. . . . [I] awakened for some reason to see seven strange looking forms at the foot of my bed—approximately 4 feet tall, large black eyes round shaped, greyish white skin, large head, very thin body, long arms, fingers and toes. They then seemed to raise me out of the bed without touching me and stayed below up the stairs and outside. There was a very bright light coming down from the sky which seemed to draw us up into it. Next thing I saw was being in a very sterile white room lying on a table with these beings around me again.

The Aliens' Appearance

Lincoln's description of her captors is similar to those of other abductees. When asked to draw the aliens, many people begin by sketching enormous black eyes in large heads. These eyes are usually almond-shaped with no pupils, irises, or corneas. Most abductees say that aliens have no eyelids and cannot blink. However, abductee Whitley Strieber insists he did see eyelids. In his book *Communion: A True Story*, he says: "I saw the huge, glassy structures recede and loosen, becoming wrinkled, and the lids come down and up at the same time, to close just below the middle of the eyeball."

The rest of an alien face appears to be less impressive. Judy Kendall tells Budd Hopkins, in his book *Missing Time*:

> [Alien heads] look like ordinary people's heads, but they don't have any hair. No hair anywhere. Their cheekbones are funny-looking. [Their skin is] kind of white and milky. . . . I don't remember seeing a mouth. . . . I don't see any ears . . . all I see is holes.

No abductee remembers seeing alien ears, but some describe a humanlike nose or a slightly raised bump where the nose should be. Many tell of mouths that are either slitlike with no lips or O-shaped with

Abductees' sketches of the aliens they have encountered often exhibit similar qualities: large heads, enormous black eyes, and slitlike mouths.

very thin lips. Few abductees see the mouth open, but those who do have noticed a membrane inside. In any case, the mouth does not seem to be used for talking. Almost all abductees say that aliens communicate telepathically, mind to mind.

As for alien chins, abductees describe them as small and pointy with no evidence of jaws. Aliens also appear to have no chewing muscles or throat movement. David Jacobs mentions one abductee who grabbed an alien by the throat and "reported that the neck seemed solid, as if it contained material inside, but it did not have the feel of moving muscles."

Abductees say that alien arms are long and thin and describe hands with some kind of thumb but only three fingers. Some abductees have seen dark, clawlike nails on alien hands while others insist there are no nails at all. Alien legs are apparently thin and straight, the exact same size at the top as at the bottom. Abductees cannot describe alien feet, and none remember seeing any toes.

Abductees have noticed that aliens lack any blemishes or irregular patches on their skin. Aliens appear to be one uniform color, usually some shade of gray but occasionally tan. Their clothing sometimes looks the same as their skin, making it hard to tell whether they are wearing anything at all.

"Incredibly Large Black Eyes"

Abductee Laurie Watkins offers a common description of the aliens when she tells Kenneth Ring:

> I saw between 6-10 figures walking near us. They were walking (floating) on a very slight incline. They were small (about the size of a 2-3 year old). They were greyish-silver (skin color) with very large heads, incredibly large black eyes, small mouths. They were wearing something like a long greyish garment (I can't remember seeing feet).

Abductees place aliens in one of two distinct physical categories. One type is small, from two to

"It is my belief that what we have here is not a wide, irregular collection of various UFO abduction accounts, each equipped with its own degree of credibility. Instead, we are seeing a wide variety of *human response* to the same, basic unearthly experience. . . . The abductees vary more than the abduction process itself."

Budd Hopkins, *Missing Time*

"Extraordinary claims require extraordinarily convincing evidence to support them if they are to be accepted as fact. . . . [Ufologists] were mistaking the *repetition* of extraordinary claims for *extraordinarily convincing evidence* to support those claims. In so doing, they were demonstrating the validity of Francis Bacon's sage observation: 'A credulous man is a deceiver.'"

Philip Klass, *UFO Abductions*

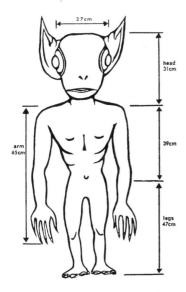

27cm

head
31cm

arm
65cm

39cm

legs
47cm

A sketch of a goblinlike alien supposedly seen in Kentucky in 1955.

just over four feet tall. The other is closer to five feet tall. The skin of the smaller aliens has a plastic quality, like a dolphin's skin, while the taller aliens appear rough and leathery. Both groups are physically inferior to human beings. Abductees say that the aliens' strength lies not in their bodies but in their ability to control the human mind and consequently the human body.

While abductees cannot tell one small alien from another, they are able to identify individuals among the taller beings. They say that the taller aliens have more character in their faces and appear to be the leaders. The taller ones sometimes wear special clothing, like a white, gray, or black laboratory coat, and direct the work of smaller aliens during physical examinations.

The Physical Examination

Abductees say the small aliens function as a group to carry out their duties. They perform the more menial tasks, such as transporting abductees to the spaceship. Both they and the tall aliens work in a businesslike manner and will not be distracted. They ignore human protests but sometimes calm people by staring into their eyes for a prolonged period of time. Abductees say this staring makes them feel very peaceful and seems to eliminate any pain caused by a medical procedure.

Nonetheless, most abductees are upset by the examinations. In *The Omega Project*, Claire Chambers, a thirty-one-year-old writer, tells Kenneth Ring:

> My boy friend (age 35) and I were both removed from my bedroom in the night. My large dog attacked and injured one of the aliens. I fought also, but was rendered unconscious. I awoke (in the craft I assume) in a strange environment lying on a table helpless with total paralysis. One alien was by my head and attempted to frighten me with his large eyes. Three other aliens were working on my body. I was terrified

and in great pain from the physical procedures they were doing to my body. At one point, I almost strangled and choked to death. I screamed, "NO! STOP! WHY?" over and over. There was no response from the alien lifeforms.

Examinations take place in small, circular rooms with strange machines, metallic-looking floors, and white and gray walls. Sometimes abductees begin their experience sitting in a narrow, curved waiting room with benches in the walls.

"I Couldn't Move a Muscle"

Aliens usually begin their examinations at the feet and work their way up, leaving no area untouched. Aliens scrape human skin for cell samples, snip off pieces of hair, and look inside eyes, ears, nose, and throat. Sometimes they use machinery similar to X-ray equipment. Abductee Tom Murillo tells Kenneth Ring:

> I was raised up into the spacecraft . . . where I landed on a glass-like table. I lay [there] for a few moments till these four tall aliens came into the room. They observed me for a while, then started their examination on me. A scanning device was used all the time. This device went around the glass table—above, sideways, under the table—and all the time I couldn't move a muscle except my eyes. All the data picked up by the scanning device was fed into a strange-shaped grey screen where I was fortunate to see my insides. My heart, my stomach, and other parts. I just lay there as I was examined.

Many abductees report that the aliens end the examination by placing a small, round object deep inside their nose or ear. Sometimes they remove an object instead. David Jacobs says that this implant has some kind of important purpose. It "might be a locator so that the targeted individual can be found and abducted; it might serve as a monitor of hormonal changes; it might facilitate the molecular changes needed for transport and entrance; it might facilitate

Many abductees report having been subjected to painful physical examinations by their captors.

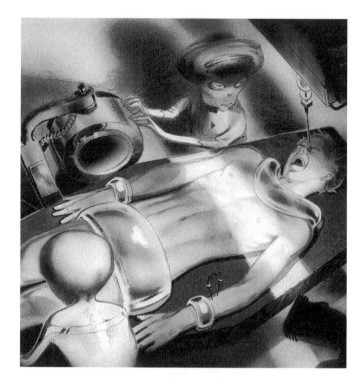

communication." Many ufologists believe the implants are tagging devices similar to the one earth scientists use to track animals for a long-term study.

Some abductees do claim to have been abducted more than once. Repeat abductees often report that the same tall alien has been present at every one of their abductions and seems to monitor anything that has changed since the last abduction. For example, one abductee tells Jacobs that the aliens showed concern when she dyed her hair from black to blonde. Another says that the aliens were puzzled after she got braces on her teeth; they removed a sample of tissue from her gum.

Abductees say aliens usually take tissue samples from the leg, arm, or back. The incisions can be long and thin, wide and messy, or scoop shaped. In addition, several male abductees report having their sperm collected, and some female abductees report that the aliens either extract ova or implant embryos that are removed during a later abduction.

Hybrid Children

Many abductees also insist they have seen half-human, half-alien children among the aliens. Some of these hybrids are fetuses in incubators that look like fish tanks with blue liquid in them. Others are young children in a nursery with four or five aliens caring for them.

Most abductees who have seen these hybrids report that they are listless and sickly. Several abductees say that the aliens want them to hold the children because the hybrids need a human's touch. One abductee tells Jacobs: "It's very important, and [the aliens] can't do it. [The child] needs it from me. [The aliens] can't give it what it needs completely. It's sort of a species-specific need, I guess."

An abductee holds a half-alien, half-human baby. Many abductees believe hybrid children need a human's touch to stay alive.

"The events recounted by a variety of people from scattered places are strikingly similar, suggesting that there might be more to the whole business than mere coincidence. In different years, different people from different parts of the country all report nearly identical [abduction] experiences. All of these people seem quite ordinary in the psychological sense . . . yet they report details of the experience that are startling in their similarity."

Dr. Aphrodite Clamar, a psychologist, in *Missing Time*

"Those [similar abduction] details don't point to anything more than a common mental experience, not unlike parasitosis, the belief you're being infested by parasites. Medical history documents that people who suffer from parasitosis reported the same parasites and drew the same drawings, with the same details. Given an infinite variety of stimulations, the brain responds in a finite number of ways."

Ronald K. Siegel, an associate research professor of psychiatry and biobehavioral sciences at UCLA, in *Omni* magazine

Some abductees report that the aliens encouraged them to play with the children, talk to them, or hold them. In his book *Abduction*, John Mack reports:

> Periodically the abductee mothers and fathers are brought to see the hybrid offspring and encouraged to hold and love them . . . [and] the abductees are naturally filled with conflict at the prospect of forming a deep bond with an odd offspring that they can only see rarely at the pleasure of the alien beings.

Abductee descriptions of the children vary greatly. Some babies seem more human, some more alien, but in every instance the infant is clearly a mixture of both species. In her book *Abducted!*, Debbie Jordan describes the child she believes was made using one of her ova:

> The little girl was about the height of a four-year-old child, but she was very tiny otherwise. She had tiny ears, set low on her head, a tiny mouth, and large blue eyes. Her forehead was very large and her body seemed very thin and frail. She had snow white hair that was patchy on her large head and her complexion was very pale. . . . [When she blinked, her] eyeballs rolled back and her eyelids met in the middle of her eyes.

Psychological Tests

Some abductees have not seen any children. Their abduction experiences center around alien psychological tests. They say that the aliens made them watch scenes on a screen or visualize scenes in their minds that evoked an emotional response, either disturbing or pleasant. During the procedure, a tall alien stared into their eyes, apparently to study their reactions.

One abductee told David Jacobs that the aliens made her visualize her mother's death. She said that during this visualization, an alien was "telling me that I [had] to feel the way I did then. . . . It [was] very emotional, and he [was] making me watch it . . . like it [was] just all happening again."

The aliens conduct other tests as well. Some of these tests determine manual dexterity. Others evaluate memory. A few examine the human pain threshold. In addition, some abductees claim that the aliens have transferred knowledge into their brains. However, these abductees cannot recall the knowledge. They say it has been hidden for future use.

The Abduction Experience Ends

Once all the tests are done, the abduction experience ends abruptly. Most abductees say that the aliens rushed them from the spacecraft to return them to the site of their abduction. Sometimes this process happens so quickly that the abductee ends up in a slightly different place.

At this point, most abductees forget their experience. Budd Hopkins believes this forgetfulness serves to protect an alien research study. In his book *Missing Time* he says:

> Memory blocks may . . . have to do with the abductee's role as a "human specimen" unwittingly being studied over a period of years. If people are being picked up as children, implanted with monitoring devices, and abducted a second time after puberty, at the very least the first abduction would have to be concealed. If the study is truly long range, the subjects would have to be kept in the dark about their role for many years, and a strongly effective block would have to be imposed.

Like Budd Hopkins, many people believe the abduction experience is real because abductee descriptions are similar, consistent, and full of detail. However, skeptics still challenge them, saying only physical proof is irrefutable. Many ufologists are therefore trying to find hard evidence that aliens exist.

Three

The Search for Physical Proof

(Opposite page) An eleven-year-old Russian girl holds a drawing of a spaceship she supposedly saw in 1989. As investigators strive to uncover the mysteries of alien abductions, they look for physical proof that aliens are indeed visiting the earth.

Ufologists want to find definite proof of alien abduction. To achieve this goal, they have studied abductees' minds as well as their bodies. In addition, they have examined the locations of UFO sightings, hoping to find evidence that alien spacecraft are indeed visiting earth.

Polygraph Examinations

Researchers often administer a polygraph examination to find out whether a particular abductee is telling the truth. A polygraph, or lie detector, examination uses a machine to detect certain changes in the human body that occur when a person is lying.

When abductee Whitley Strieber took such a test and answered questions about his abduction experience, the results indicated he was not lying about having had a close encounter of the fourth kind. However, as Strieber himself admits in his book *Communion*, a polygraph examination does not prove an abduction has really taken place. It merely shows that the abductee *believes* it has taken place. Strieber states: "My successful completion of this test in no way proves that my recollection of my experiences is correct, but it does confirm that I have described what I saw to the best of my ability."

"Physical evidence is important to corroborate the experiencers' reports. But if taken out of this context, the physical phenomena are rarely sufficiently robust to stand in their own right. If, for example, I were to publish photographs of skin lesions . . . obtained . . . in the same night [as a reported abduction] . . . I would, as a physician, be leaving myself open to legitimate criticism by dermatologists that I could not prove that they were directly related to the abduction experiences and not caused by other factors."

John Mack, *Abduction*

"To my knowledge we have yet to recover an implant that resembles anything alien. Instead, the chances of somebody finding a little something wrong with his or her body are greater than we think. Statistically, if you look at the population at large, you are going to see a lot of people who have had growths and bumps and pieces of stuff stuck in their body."

William Cone, a psychologist, in *Omni* magazine

In addition to the polygraph examination, researchers sometimes administer psychological tests to determine an abductee's mental stability. The results of such tests have led some psychologists to conclude that most abductees are surprisingly normal. For example, Dr. Aphrodite Clamar, who interviewed the abductees mentioned in Budd Hopkins's book *Missing Time*, says she discovered nothing unusual about any of Hopkins's subjects. She states:

> I did not find any drug users among the subjects whom Budd Hopkins brought, nor any alcoholism, nor any strange habits. . . . Persons who claim to have had UFO experiences . . . come in all sizes, shapes, ages, and sexes. . . . [They] are run-of-the-mill people, neither psycho nor psychic, people like you and me. I could find no common thread that ties them together—other than their UFO experience—and no common pathology; indeed, no discernible pathology at all.

Nonetheless, skeptics still insist that abductees are mentally unbalanced. They remind us that these people often have emotional problems, which psychologists label postabduction syndrome. Skeptics do not think PAS comes from being abducted; they believe it is a sign of a hidden psychological disorder that actually causes the sufferer to *think* he or she has been abducted.

Physical Signs

However, abductees who claim to have experienced alien surgical procedures do exhibit scars on their bodies. Many ufologists say this proves without doubt that alien abductions are real. Physicians cannot explain these scars, which sometimes seem surgically precise and can appear inside the nose or within other internal organs.

Some of these scars are quite unusual. In his book *The Omega Project*, Kenneth Ring recounts the story of one abductee who exhibited marks the day after experiencing an alien medical procedure. This woman explains:

> Under closer examination I noticed that they were three small blisters in the shape of a triangle. It really frightened my husband and me. I couldn't concentrate on anything all day. Later that night when taking my bath I noticed that the blisters had dried up somewhat and turned black. (Now they are still visible like burn scars.)

Skeptic Philip Klass believes such scars were caused by long-forgotten, ordinary childhood events. But Kenneth Ring argues that the human mind could be creating them. Researchers know that people can control their blood pressure and other bodily functions through mental techniques like biofeedback and meditation. More importantly, followers of the Christian religion sometimes exhibit spontaneously occurring wounds, called stigmata, on their hands and feet. These Christians believe their wounds were made by God to remind them of Jesus Christ's crucifixion. Nonbelievers say stigmata are proof that human thought can affect skin tissue.

Alien Implants

Skin tissue changes might account for another physical sign of abduction—alien implants. Some abductees claim they have found the implants that aliens have placed within their bodies. One abductee, Richard Price, says an implant worked its way loose from his skin in June 1989. He gave this object to David Pritchard, a scientist at the Massachusetts Institute of Technology.

Pritchard analyzed the object and reluctantly decided it was not alien in nature. In the April 1995 issue of *Omni* magazine, in an article entitled "Alien Implant or—Human Underwear?" by Patrick Huyghe, Pritchard states that the object was made of "the kind of material elements and chemicals—carbon, oxygen, hydrogen, and compounds—one would expect if the object were biological in origin and formed right here on planet Earth."

Dermatopathologist Thomas Flotte, an expert in skin diseases from Massachusetts General Hospital in Boston, agrees. He says the human body itself is capable of producing such an object. Author Huyghe explains:

> Thomas Flotte found that the "implant" consists of concentric layers of fibroblasts, a type of cell found in connective tissue, extracellular material like collagen, and some external cotton fibers [that came from Price's clothing and became incorporated into the tissue as it hardened]. The human body apparently produces such calcified tissue in response to injury, either from foreign material like a piece of glass or a wood splinter, or from a trauma of some kind, caused perhaps by a baseball or a table corner.

Huyghe suggests that the cotton fibers came from the fabric of Price's underwear and "became incorporated into the body tissue as it hardened."

Still, Pritchard thinks that aliens *could* have made the object. He says:

> It's possible that the aliens are so clever that they can make devices that serve their purposes yet appear to have a prosaic origin as natural products of the human body and fibers from cotton underwear. So this case only rules out the possibility of clumsy aliens. It doesn't rule out the possibility of super-clever aliens.

Photographic Evidence

With skeptics dismissing proof gathered from the minds and bodies of abductees, ufologists have turned elsewhere for evidence of alien contact. They have produced photographs of flying alien spacecraft to show that UFOs exist. However, in every instance, skeptics insist the photographs are hoaxes.

According to Donald H. Menzel and Ernest H. Taves in their book *The UFO Enigma: The Defini-*

tive Explanation of the UFO Phenomenon, UFO photographs are easy to fake. They say:

> One need not be an expert in trick photography to produce realistic but phony pictures of UFOs. This has been accomplished repeatedly in recent years by wily young children, aided by the fact that many natural objects closely resemble the conventional concept of an UFO: a garbage-can lid, the top of a cigar humidifier, a lens cap, a Frisbee, and even a straw hat.

Fake UFO photographs are indeed common, but they are not all produced by people trying to prove that UFOs exist. Other people, called debunkers, use them to trick ufologists. Ed and Frances Walters, in their book *UFO Abductions in Gulf Breeze*, explain that a debunker is "a person who will create false evidence in an effort to distort and discredit

This 1967 photo was taken in California through the window of a truck. Is it a hoax? Investigators found that by hanging a camera lens cap just a few inches outside the truck window a very similar picture is produced.

UFO sightings, especially UFO photo evidence." If a debunker can get a ufologist to say that a fake UFO photo is real, that debunker can then expose the fake and destroy the ufologist's credibility. According to the Walters, "motivated UFO debunkers go to a lot of trouble in their efforts to ridicule the UFO phenomenon. Discrediting real UFO photographs with their fake photographs is a common practice used by debunkers to influence negative stories in the media."

Ufologists therefore examine any UFO photographs they receive from the public very carefully. They use computers to analyze UFO images for hidden strings, unusual shadows, or other evidence of fakery. Over the years, the equipment for such electronic analysis has become more sophisticated. Many ufologists now feel confident about declaring some UFO photographs authentic.

However, given the thousands of UFOs sighted in the sky each year, skeptics say that if UFOs are real there should be more than just a few authentic photographs of them. Ed Walters disagrees, arguing that most people do not carry a camera with them at times when they would see a UFO. He explains:

> We could equate the odds of seeing a UFO to the possibility of seeing an automobile accident or some other newsmaking event and realizing that you don't have a camera with you. . . . [Actually] I am impressed with the number of quality photographs that have been taken.

Gulf Breeze, Florida

In addition to appearing in photographs, UFOs have also been captured on videotape. An ABC news crew filmed a UFO in the skies over Gulf Breeze, Florida, on January 11, 1991. Another was filmed over Gulf Breeze on May 10, 1991, by a Japanese crew from the NIPON television network.

UFOs have been videotaped in other places besides Florida. For example, in Mexico City, Mexico,

"For much less than a million dollars one could easily build an object that would look like a flying saucer and would hover in appropriate fashion long enough for someone to take photographs of it."

Jacques Vallee, *Revelations*

"I have tried to consider all the options to this Gulf Breeze mystery. I would like to explain it away as a military aircraft, balloons, flares, temperature inversions, or hoax, but none of these options hold up under scientific study."

Bob Oeschsler, former NASA systems specialist, in *UFO Abductions in Gulf Breeze*

GULF BREEZE

on New Year's Day in 1993 several witnesses, including a Catholic priest, videotaped a group of UFOs. However, Gulf Breeze is one of the most repeatedly photographed UFO sites. Ufologists call the entire gulf-strip area a "UFO hot spot," because it boasts an unusually large number of sightings. Other hot spots in the United States are the Pacific Northwest and the Texas and New Mexico regions.

In Gulf Breeze, both individuals and groups have sighted UFOs. Witnesses include police officers, local government officials, and a retired air force F-4 pilot. This pilot described his sighting in the March 30, 1989, edition of a Gulf Breeze newspaper, the *Sentinel*:

> I was able to snap 3 photos in rapid succession
> before the object departed to the west. I'm not

Skeptical ufologist Philip Klass stands beside a display of Gulf Breeze UFO photos. Numerous UFOs have been photographed or videotaped over the entire gulf-strip area.

sure what I photographed but it wasn't one of our local aircraft. This thing made no noise and climbed away like a rocket. My truck would not start for about 5 minutes after the object left and I noticed that I had built up a pretty stout static electric charge when I touched the door handle.

Gulf Breeze is also the reported site of an abduction experience. Ed Walters says that after an episode of missing time he underwent hypnosis and recalled being abducted from the community several times. According to Walters, the aliens placed a strange apparatus on his head that made him recall certain events in his life. He explains: "The visions were rapid and took me on an emotional roller coaster ride. . . . For reasons unknown to me, I was being forced to relive experiences in my life which involved intense emotion." Walters says that the aliens triggered "four different feelings perhaps unique to humans, Joy, Love, Grief, and Pride."

Walters has no doubt that his abduction experience really happened. He is frustrated when people say they don't believe him. After all, he argues, he has taken many photographs of UFOs flying over Gulf Breeze. Is this not definite proof that aliens have visited his community?

Fake UFO Photographs?

Skeptics have called Ed Walters a liar and claim to have solid evidence that his UFO photographs are a hoax. In 1990, a reporter covering a Mutual UFO Network (MUFON) International Symposium on the Gulf Breeze phenomenon found a model of a spaceship at Ed Walters's former home. Skeptics suggest that Walters used this model to fake Gulf Breeze UFO photographs.

Walters insists that the model is the wrong size and shape to produce the UFOs seen in the photographs. He says that debunkers manufactured the model themselves. However, in his book *Revelations: Alien Contact and Human Deception*, skeptic

Ed Walters claims to have been abducted by aliens several times in the Gulf Breeze area, and he says he has photographs of the alien spaceship to prove it. Skeptics have called the photos a hoax.

Jacques Vallee, attacks Walters's reputation and calls the entire Gulf Breeze phenomenon "sleazy." The publicity resulting from the area's UFOs has led Vallee to believe that Walters and other residents manufactured the photographs to make their community famous.

Mysterious Grass Circles

But Walters says his photographs are not the only proof that UFOs have landed near his home. Gulf Breeze is also the site of several mysteriously flattened grass circles, long thought by ufologists to be a possible sign of alien contact. Walters saw one of them himself and reports: "The long grass within the circle refused to stand up and weeks later, even after a flood of spectators and scientists, the swirled grass remained growing in a clockwise circle."

Such circles often occur in tandem with UFO sightings and have appeared in fields of grass or crops all over the world. In his book *UFO: The Complete Sightings*, Peter Brookesmith describes these circles:

> At the beginning of the decade people found only plain circles. Their sizes ranged from the diameter of a cartwheel to that of a circus arena. In these formations, a typical pattern can be seen in the bent crops: an outward swirling of the stalks, interwoven layers of stalks, twisted straws and, occasionally, a centre with crops still standing. As the years passed, the phenomenon developed into circles with rings around them, or consisting entirely of rings. There were several symmetrically placed circles, or single large ones with minor, precisely aligned "satellites."

Crop-circle researcher Colin Andrews reveals that some of these crop circles have been faked. In his article "Full Circle" in *International UFO Library* magazine, he states that many hoaxes occurred after news of the phenomenon became widespread in 1989. Since then, several people have

Curious tourists walk through mysterious crop circles discovered in an England field in 1990. Are the circles a form of alien communication?

stepped forward to say they made the crop circles themselves.

In September 1991, Douglas Bower and David Chorley took credit for hundreds of crop circles that appeared in southern England after 1978. They explained that they had used wooden boards and twine to press down crops without leaving any footprints. In the United States, some Iowa farmers made the same claim. Debunkers say these stories are proof that the entire crop-circle phenomenon is a hoax.

Nonetheless, researchers say that human beings cannot possibly be responsible for all of the crop circles that appear throughout the world. Peter Brookesmith states: "Bower and Chorley never claimed to have made any of the pre-1978 circles already on record. Nor could they—or any of the other hoaxers who have since come forward—have made the many hundreds of circles seen elsewhere in the world."

Crop-circle researchers add that no one has yet been able to duplicate the exact characteristics of the most mysterious crop circles. Colin Andrews believes that almost all pre-1989 crop circles exhibit patterns that cannot be reproduced by human beings. He hopes that subsequent hoaxes will not end interest in the genuine phenomenon.

Nonalien Explanations

However, he and other crop-circle experts also say that there are several nonalien explanations for the phenomenon. Some researchers suspect that the earth's magnetism is somehow responsible. Others think it is caused by a combination of the wind and electrical effects. Peter Brookesmith explains:

> According to Professors John Snow and Tokio Kikuchi, when eddies of wind "break down," they move towards the ground and sweep out circles in the crops. Professor G. Terence Meaden has suggested that, as this happens, friction in the moving air separates and concentrates existing electrical charges in the atmosphere. This accounts for the humming noises and for the sometimes spectacular lights [that witnesses have said were UFOs].

Professor Stephen Hawking, one of the world's most renowned scientists, also believes that crop circles are made by natural vortices, or currents, in the earth's atmosphere. However, some people argue that genuine circle groupings are too intricate to have been made by natural forces. They are certain that these circles are a form of alien communication. Brookesmith reports:

> Some observers regarded the circles as coded mystical messages from the Earth's "consciousness." Others stuck to a more traditional interpretation. One of these was engineer Pat Delgado who suggested: "Maybe

"These crop sculptures are too perfect to have been created by humans with tools and they are too perfect to have been created by natural weather occurrences. . . . Someone is leaving messages in fields and I want to know why and what they mean. . . . We finally have physical proof that aliens exist and it is time to investigate the evidence."

J. Case of Arizona, in a letter to the editors of *Omni* magazine

"That UFOs have been seen at around the same time that crop circles have been created, is not in doubt. The question of whether the crop circles involve any form of 'alien intelligence' is another matter entirely."

Peter Brookesmith, *UFO: The Complete Sightings*

Could this circular indentation in a beanfield in Iowa be the landing site of a UFO that was spotted in the area?

these circles are created by alien beings using forcefields unknown to us. They may be manipulating existing Earth energy."

A Different Kind of Circle

Crop circles are not the only kind of circle associated with UFOs. In locations where abductees say a spaceship has landed, sometimes the ground appears damaged. This damage is also in the form of a circle.

In her book *Abducted!*, Kathy Mitchell says that after a UFO appeared in her backyard, she saw "an eight-foot circle of dead grass . . . with a swath of dead grass coming from the circle in a perfectly straight path that was approximately two feet wide and forty-eight feet long." Mitchell says that the circle remained "unchanged after months of fertilizing, watering, and reseeding" and lasted for five years, during which time all animals avoided it. She adds that "the ground inside the circle and strip repelled not only water, but any new life, including weeds. . . . The dirt in the affected area was like ground-up cement."

Investigating the Circle

Budd Hopkins investigated this circle. He photographed it and took two soil samples from Mitchell's yard, one from inside the circle and one from outside it. He sent both samples to a laboratory for analysis. The laboratory then tried to make the normal soil match the damaged soil by subjecting it to extreme heat.

In his book *Intruders:The Incredible Visitations at Copley Woods*, Hopkins reports:

> It was necessary to heat the unaffected sample in an oven at 800 degrees Fahrenheit for six hours to achieve the same color as that of the affected soil, though without duplicating its solidified appearance. Clearly, the amount of energy emitted by something [at the location of the circle] was enormous, though we have no idea of its nature.

However, Philip Klass says this circle might have been caused by nothing more than a simple fungus:

> Some centuries earlier, the visible aftermath of this fungus, which dehydrates the soil so nothing will grow there and which often takes on an irregular circular shape, was given the name "Fairy Ring" because some superstitious folk assumed that it was a playground for tiny fairies. Today, for many UFOlogists, such Fairy Rings have become the mark of UFO landing-sites.

The fungus theory cannot explain a similar circle that appeared in Medford, Minnesota, in November 1975, however. At that time, the Kay family reported that a UFO had landed at a nearby football field. Investigators later examined the area and took soil samples from the landing site. These samples were analyzed at the University of Kansas Space Technology Laboratory.

According to Peter Brookesmith, the landing-site samples "showed a level of thermo-luminescence that was 10 times higher than that of control samples taken from near the site." In other words, the affected soil emitted ten times more heat and light than the normal soil. However, it looked the same as the normal soil when viewed under a microscope.

Mysterious Cattle Mutilations

Ufologists say that unusual soil at landing sites is not the only indication that aliens might be visiting earth. Some suggest a connection exists between UFOs and some mysterious cattle mutilations that have occurred throughout the world.

In his book *Extra-Terrestrials Among Us*, George C. Andrews reports there have been more than ten thousand cases of cattle mutilations in the United States alone. Butchered carcasses are frequently discovered in the vicinity of a previous UFO sighting. Andrews describes one cow as having been "cut open by something that left neatly and precisely defined serrated edges. Two different medical pathologists certified that this could not be attributed to predators or barbed wire."

Andrews adds that these mutilations share certain characteristics:

> Typically, only reproductive and digestive organs that we consider inedible are taken, perhaps with an ear or an eye or the tongue. Carcasses have frequently been found drained of almost every last drop of blood in a way that would be impossible even with the use of a powerful vacuum pump, as normally the veins would collapse before all the blood could be extracted. Such carcasses often had two puncture wounds in the throat.

Skeptics believe the mutilations could have been caused by coyotes or other predators. But witnesses say such predators often go out of their way to avoid the mutilated carcasses. Coyotes in particular will not go near them.

There are other facts that suggest a predator is not involved. Peter Brookesmith describes one 1993 case:

Even the victims' capillary veins were emptied, which is not the case in animals wounded by predators. Microscopic examination revealed that haemoglobin in the remaining flesh was often cooked, indicating that a laser-like heat source generating temperatures of at least 300° F (149° C) had been used to cut it, but without leaving the carbon traces normally deposited by lasers.

A 1978 photo shows a cattle mutilation that occurred in New Hampshire. The puzzling mutilation cases, which have been discovered around the world, have left many wondering if extraterrestrials are responsible.

Some people think that cattle mutilations are the work of human beings. But just as with grass and crop circles, there are no tracks, human or otherwise, leading to the sites. Several ufologists say this absence of tracks means UFOs could be involved.

Animal Abductions

A few abductees say they know aliens are mutilating the cattle. These people claim to have witnessed alien surgical procedures on the animals. George Andrews describes the experience of one such abductee:

Mrs. [Judy] Doraty was driving through Texas with members of her family, when she noticed that a UFO was following her car. She saw a calf being sucked up toward the UFO through a beam of light. Next she found herself aboard the UFO with her daughter, watching "little men" cut up the calf. She was terrified when the "little men" began examining her daughter on what looked like an operating table, but she and her daughter were returned to the ground safely.

However, Andrews adds that mysterious black helicopters with human pilots have sometimes been seen immediately before or after the discovery of the carcasses. Could the phenomenon have an earthly cause after all?

Andrews suggests that the helicopters could be the property of the U.S. government. He believes the U.S. military might be mutilating the cattle. To support this belief, he quotes from an anonymous letter published in a Denver newspaper on April 8, 1983, that begins:

I was in the Army, stationed in New Mexico. Got out in '81. I was in Intelligence, and learned what's really going on. I trust you won't print my name, or I'll be dead within a year. The mutilations are done by a secret government operation called Delta. . . . They take the animals parts to test the effects of germ warfare and poison (some weak mix of cyanide and dioxin) they're testing on the civilians in America.

Andrews favors the idea of government involvement over the possibility that a private organization is responsible for the mutilations. He explains:

> Since many mutilations have occurred near air bases and sensitive military installations thoroughly covered by long-range radar, where any intruding civilian helicopter pilot would have been immediately challenged by jet fighters, it is difficult to believe that the military didn't know what was going on.

Andrews is not alone in believing the U.S. government could be hiding information from the American public. Many ufologists think the military is keeping secrets not only about the cause of cattle mutilations but about the reality of UFOs. They are convinced that the government has actual UFO spacecraft parts and alien bodies hidden in secret military installations throughout the United States.

Four

Is the U.S. Government Hiding Evidence of Alien Contact?

The United States Freedom of Information Act gives American citizens the right to know a great deal about their government's activities. However, it also acknowledges the president's right to keep certain matters secret. The act states that information does not have to be made public for "matters that are . . . specifically authorized under criteria established by an Executive order to be kept secret in the interest of national defense or foreign policy." In other words, the public can be denied access to information because a presidential executive order has designated that information as restricted, or "classified."

Although the act lists several more reasons a document might be classified, ufologists are interested in the section involving national defense. The U.S. military advises the president on defense issues, and ufologists believe the military has evidence that aliens are real. Could the military be encouraging the president to withhold information about UFOs from the American people?

Roswell

Many popular books, movies, and television programs suggest this is the case. For example, in 1994 Viacom Pictures released the movie *Roswell*,

(Opposite page) Brigadier General Roger Ramey and Colonel Thomas Dubose of the U.S. Air Force identify metallic fragments of a crashed UFO found near Roswell, New Mexico, in 1947. The secrecy surrounding the famous Roswell incident led many people to suspect that the U.S. government is hiding evidence of alien contact.

which shows massive government deception involving UFOs. The movie depicts a real, but highly controversial, event.

A Strange Discovery

On July 2, 1947, there was a violent thunderstorm in the area around the army airfield at Roswell, New Mexico. During the storm, rancher Mac Brazel heard a loud crash near his home, and the next day he discovered hundreds of small pieces of a strange material that looked a little like tinfoil in one of his fields. Some of the pieces were shaped like I-beams, which are horizontal girders used in building construction.

A scene from the movie *Roswell* depicts military intelligence agent Jesse Marcel at the site of the downed UFO.

Brazel picked up one of the pieces. It was extremely lightweight and thin, but he could not bend it, cut it, or burn it. It was not tinfoil. He suspected it might have come from the crash of an experimental military aircraft.

Brazel took a few pieces to the local sheriff, who called officials at the airfield. Officers sent two military intelligence agents to investigate the matter.

When agent Jesse A. Marcel arrived at the crash site, he concluded that the amount of the debris indicated that it had indeed come from something large. However, he knew the source could not have been a military craft because human technology was incapable of producing material that was so light and thin but unbendable. He hit it with a sledgehammer and found it did not dent. He lit it and discovered it would not burn. In addition, one of the pieces had strange geometric writing on it.

"Nothing from the Earth"

In their book *UFO Crash at Roswell*, Kevin Randle and Donald Schmitt explain Marcel's thoughts about the debris:

> Interviewed over thirty years after the event, Marcel said, without any qualification, that the material was "nothing from the Earth." He said that because of his training, and his position as an air intelligence officer, he was familiar with all types of aircraft, rockets, balloons, and even the top secret experiments that were being conducted in New Mexico. Given all that, he still didn't know what he had seen that day north of Roswell. He went to his grave believing that he had held the pieces of spacecraft from another planet.

Marcel collected samples of the debris and took them back to the military base. When Marcel's superior officers saw it, they took action. They sent troops to surround the crash site and keep other people away. Then they ordered Marcel to accompany

"That something, which the military establishment wanted to keep very secret, came down from the sky [near Roswell, New Mexico] that night seems beyond doubt. But the evidence will fit several scenarios, none involving extraterrestrial craft or aliens."

Peter Brookesmith, *UFO: The Complete Sightings*

"I know that some kind of nonhuman intelligence is interacting with us, but on its own terms, telling us only what it wishes to, and manipulating us with cold objectivity. I also know that some part of our government is aware of these intrusions and depredations but for its own reasons is deliberately denying this fact to the public at large."

Budd Hopkins, in *Abducted!*

his samples to Fort Worth, Texas, where soldiers would transfer them to another plane bound for the Intelligence Center at Wright-Patterson Air Force Base in Dayton, Ohio.

A Military Secret

The local army officers hoped to keep the entire incident a secret. However, rancher Brazel and the sheriff had already told friends about it. Their story was spreading quickly, and the officers feared the media would soon invade the crash site. They ordered their public information officer, First Lieutenant Walter Haut, to confirm that an alien spaceship had indeed crashed in the desert. But he was to tell the press that the military had already taken the ship to Fort Worth.

Reporters immediately raced to Fort Worth to get pictures of the spaceship. When they got there, the military allowed them to photograph some debris. The next day the military announced that the officers at Roswell had been mistaken and that the debris they had photographed was from an ordinary weather balloon.

Marcel says that the military deliberately replaced his debris with the weather balloon pieces to convince the press that no aliens existed. It was a cover-up, and it worked. When people looked at the photographs, they could see that the pieces were made of ordinary material. The Roswell story soon died.

According to Marcel, the government ordered him not to tell anybody what he had really found at the crash site. He says rancher Brazel and the sheriff agreed to cooperate, and the matter was immediately classified top secret.

Alien Bodies

However, there were other witnesses to the event. While Marcel was still in Fort Worth, military personnel were ordered to the crash site. They were told to truck the remaining debris back to the

Roswell airfield. Air force pilots then flew it to various military bases across the United States. No one can say what happened to the pieces after that.

However, before all the debris was transported, one officer realized that when airplanes crash, their wreckage can be scattered over several miles. He decided to order an air search of the entire region. Within a few hours, the military searchers had found a second area of debris.

They were not the first to discover it. Civil engineer Grady L. Barnett had been working three miles from the second crash site. He got there before the military. So did some student archaeologists who had been digging in the area. These people later told friends and family what they saw in the desert that day.

Major Marcel holds a piece of the foil-like material from the crashed UFO found by rancher Mac Brazel.

Though government officials deny it, some ufologists believe that Secretary of Defense James V. Forrestal communicated with an alien that landed near Roswell, New Mexico.

The witnesses said the location had a spaceship with four aliens lying on the ground beside it. The aliens were less than five feet tall and had large heads and odd, leathery skin. Most witnesses said they were all dead, but some said two were dead, one was dying, and one was seriously injured.

Some ufologists think the injured alien not only survived the crash but also later communicated with Secretary of Defense James V. Forrestal. In his article "Roswell" in *International UFO Library* magazine, Sonny Gordon states: "Forrestal was known to have kept a diary and it was rumored that he had made several entries concerning his encounter with the alien."

Other witnesses say they saw all of the aliens after they were taken to the Roswell air base hospital. A local mortician insists he got a phone call from someone asking how to preserve their bodies. Both a nurse and a pathologist claim to have personally examined dead aliens. Several military officers contend they saw the pathologist's report, which included photographs.

Air base pilots report that they eventually flew the bodies from Roswell to the Intelligence Center at Wright-Patterson Air Force Base in Dayton, Ohio, by way of Fort Worth. Like Marcel, they and other witnesses claim that the military ordered them not to talk about the aliens. Some witnesses say that the government actually threatened them with violence if they revealed what they knew.

Witnesses Come Forward

As a result, no one spoke about the Roswell incident for more than thirty years. Then Jesse Marcel learned he was dying of cancer and decided to tell reporters about his experiences while he was a military officer at Roswell. Soon other witnesses came forward. Since Marcel's death in 1986, more than 350 people have talked about seeing the aliens or their spaceships.

One of the most important witnesses is Brigadier General Arthur E. Exon. Exon was stationed at Wright-Patterson Air Force Base as a lieutenant colonel during the Roswell incident. He himself never saw the bodies or the spaceship, but he is certain they existed. Exon says he knew the men who tested the strange material. He also heard details about the alien craft and its occupants. He believes the bodies are still at Wright-Patterson.

Walter Haut, the lieutenant who reported the Roswell spacecraft to reporters, agrees. In the book *UFO Crash at Roswell*, Haut says: "I think there was one gigantic cover-up on the thing. I think that somewhere all this material is stashed away."

Both Haut and Exon believe that the military will do anything to hide what happened in New Mexico. Sonny Gordon, in his article "Roswell," supports this view. He says that former secretary of defense Forrestal may have died because of what he knew about Roswell. His diary made him a threat to military secrecy. Gordon explains: "Admitted to the Bethesda Naval Hospital for what was termed 'occupational fatigue,' he supposedly jumped to his death from his 16th floor room. Now, almost fifty years later, the diary is still considered 'Top Secret' and not allowed to be read by the public."

Brigadier General Exon says that the government created a secret intelligence group to control access to all information and materials related to the Roswell crash. He believes this group is now responsible for covering up any other evidence of UFOs. Exon thinks that the public may never learn the truth about the aliens.

A *Fu-go* Balloon

Skeptics insist that no one saw any alien bodies at Roswell. They say that the debris really was caused by a weather balloon or some other manmade object.

Skeptic John Keel theorizes that the debris was from a balloon bomb, also called a *fu-go* balloon.

Fu-go balloons were made of rice paper and filled with special incendiary devices. These bombs were sent into the air by the Japanese during World War II, which ended two years prior to the Roswell incident.

Peter Brookesmith, in his book *UFO: The Complete Sightings*, explains how such a balloon could have remained in the air for so long:

> A *fu-go* balloon was huge, filled with 19,000 cubic feet . . . of gas. The top was silvered to reflect sunlight and stop the gas overheating and lifting the balloon too high. In 1945 over 9000 of these devices were launched from Japan into the jetstream, and between 300 and 500 of the weapons reached the USA. But they could stay in the air for a very long time.

When they finally sank to earth, *fu-go* balloons could be fatal. During the war, they caused six confirmed deaths in the United States. Keel thinks the U.S. military decided to say the Roswell debris was a weather balloon so the Japanese would not know their *fu-go* balloon had finally reached its target. Official documents confirm that during the war the U.S. government intentionally concealed the fact that *fu-go* balloons had exploded on American soil.

No Reason to Lie

However, in their book *UFO Crash at Roswell*, Randle and Schmitt say that after the war, the military no longer had a reason to lie about the existence of the balloons. Randle and Schmitt also state:

> Keel never bothers with descriptions of the crash site. He dismisses the testimony of more than a half dozen witnesses who said the debris was scattered over a wide area. That was too much debris for one of the Japanese Balloon Bombs, which were about thirty feet in diameter.

But Peter Brookesmith offers additional evidence that the debris might have been from a *fu-go* balloon. He states: "Witnesses said the 'hieroglyphs' on the Roswell debris were 'like the writing on firecrackers' and were arranged in columns. They were, most likely, Japanese pictograms."

Still, Randle and Schmitt think it is ridiculous to propose that the Roswell crash involved a *fu-go* balloon. They say that anyone who suggests this idea has not given enough thought to what a *fu-go* balloon was made of. The authors explain: "Rice paper would have burned easily. . . . Rice paper would have torn and if the material was some of the rubberized stuff used on a few of the balloons, it certainly would have shown the effects of the hammer." In other words, if the debris was man-made, why was Marcel unable to dent it with his sledgehammer or set it on fire?

Jacques Vallee thinks these questions are unimportant. In his book *Revelations*, he states that human beings are quite capable of making a substance that no hammer can dent and no match can burn. He says:

> I am not very disturbed by the fact that the material found at Roswell was strong and nearly indestructible, as tested by the farmers and some of the military men. Material that can be hit with a sledgehammer without damage, yet will remain flexible and will not burn, is not beyond modern technology at all.

Human-Made Aliens

But Vallee does not think that the Roswell object was a *fu-go* balloon. He offers another explanation for the debris and bodies at Roswell. He suggests they were manufactured by the U.S. military as a way of hiding government secrets and explains:

> Roswell was the site for the very first air base equipped with atomic bombs. If a special type of balloon or drone, designed to monitor atmospheric radioactivity in the area, had been flown over New Mexico, such a device might well have been brought down during a thunderstorm. Given the extremely high sensitivity of anything related to the bomb or to

"To even question that the aliens have been captured and their craft studied by the United States government is a faux pas of gigantic proportions among UFO believers. My plain, logical questions on this topic have caused the pompous leaders of this strange discipline to regard me as the proverbial skunk spoiling their neat extraterrestrial garden party."

Jacques Vallee, *Revelations*

"The fact is, one in ten Americans claims to have seen a UFO, and more than half believe that we are not alone. The military establishment can't keep up this deceit much longer. We're becoming too aware."

Sonny Gordon, *International UFO Library* magazine

radioactivity at the time, it would have been a high priority, top secret task to recover any lost device of that type and to explain it away at all costs: as a weather balloon, as a radar test instrument, as a probe, *or even as a crashed flying saucer.* It would not have been difficult to plant an egg-shaped device in the desert to divert attention from the real debris, and even to scatter a few diminutive bodies to represent dead aliens. The Air Force had several days to do it.

Technological Information

Nonetheless, Peter Brookesmith reports that the Roswell incident fueled "the belief that the US and quite probably other governments too were aware of far more about UFOs than they had ever admitted." Many people believe that military officials did recover an alien spaceship at Roswell and have been trying to copy its technology. Several top-secret government installations are rumored to be testing sites for various alien-inspired planes and spaceships.

Other people have taken this idea one step further. They say that the government is not just researching alien devices but also getting information directly from the aliens themselves. Brookesmith says such people think "that the US government . . . actually contacted aliens and . . . concluded a deal whereby [these aliens] would be allowed a free hand in abductions and animal experiments in return for technological information."

In other words, some people believe that the United States has struck a bargain with the aliens. The government is allowing them to conduct experiments on a few select people and animals without human interference. In exchange, the aliens are supplying the U.S. military with information about their spaceship technology, inventions, medical advances, and perhaps even weapons.

People who suspect that the U.S. government is somehow involved in alien abductions offer many

"I'm getting tired of being mistaken for a weather balloon!"

reasons for this belief. They specifically cite the fact that abductees often feel they are being harassed by mysterious black helicopters. These helicopters seem similar to the ones witnessed near cattle mutilations, and many abductees suspect the aircraft are controlled by the U.S. military.

Abductee Kathy Mitchell mentions the black helicopters in her book *Abducted!*: "Mysterious black helicopters, completely devoid of any identification, are common sights around my house."

The Haley Case

An abductee who calls herself Leah A. Haley also claims to have seen these helicopters. Haley is an accountant and mother of two from Columbus,

Mississippi, who began to have disturbing dreams about aliens in 1994. She subsequently visited a psychiatrist and underwent hypnosis. Through this process, she decided that her dreams reflected a real occurrence.

Haley not only claims to have been examined by aliens but says they took her for a ride aboard their spacecraft. She says that while she was aboard, the spaceship crashed, and human military personnel helped her from the wreckage. Haley insists that this is why the military is harassing her. In an article in *Omni* magazine entitled "Anatomy of an Abduction" by A. J. S. Rayl, Haley says: "I was on that alien craft when it crashed and the military wanted to glean information and make me shut up."

Followed by Helicopters

According to Rayl, Haley has had a lot of experience with mysterious black helicopters. He says:

Since September 1990, Haley claims, she has been "followed by military types in navy blue or white cars," and occasionally by black unmarked helicopters. She also claims she has been monitored via her telephone and in person.

Tony Scarborough, a physics professor at Delta State University in Cleveland, Mississippi, confirms that Haley seems to attract black helicopters. He once saw one hover over a building where she was giving a speech on UFOs. He noticed another one a year later. This helicopter, he says, "flew at about 500 feet, traveling parallel to me on my way to meet [Haley] at Delta State University." However, he adds that this event could have been a coincidence.

Psychologist Keith Harary, research director of the Institute for Advanced Psychology in San Francisco, agrees. He told Rayl: "A string of seemingly inexplicable events that occur around the same time are not necessarily related. You would have to thoroughly investigate each and every one."

But Haley insists that government agents are harassing her, and the black helicopters offer possible evidence of this. As a result, her case has become important to all ufologists who believe the military has information about alien abductions.

Physical Signs of Alien Contact

Rayl looked for evidence that Haley is telling the truth. He reports that she has shown physical signs of possible alien contact. He says:

Haley has found "more than one hundred strange marks" on different parts of her body, including injection marks, scoop marks, and red, circular vaccinationlike marks, apparently made with three separate prongs. She also reports other physical anomalies, such as "Morse Code-type beeps" in her ears, intense back spasms, voices and imagery.

Nonetheless, Rayl admits that Haley could be causing these things herself. He quotes psychologist Keith Harary as stating:

Strange marks appearing overnight is just not that unusual, and without observing Haley close up during the times these things occur, you cannot draw any kind of valid conclusion about what's going on. We would have to rule out all conventional explanations, including, for example, the possibility that she could be doing these things to herself in an altered, or even an ordinary, state of consciousness.

But what about Haley's claims of government involvement? She specifically reports being harassed by personnel at the Columbus, Mississippi, air force base. Rayl contacted Sergeant Debbie O'Leary from the public affairs office of the base who stated: "There have been no UFOs tracked here, and we have not interrogated here any people who claim to have had an alien encounter." U.S. military personnel at Columbus say they know nothing about the Haley case.

Rayl adds that the staff of *Omni* magazine tried to verify Haley's abduction experience by checking out various names and locations she had remembered under hypnosis. However, they were unable to find any evidence that her abduction was anything other than a dream validated by hypnosis. Rayl concludes:

> Despite the fact that some UFO researchers have called the Haley case one of the most intriguing and apparently best-documented abductions ever, without more data it's impossible to know what Haley has experienced, and why. There is no hard evidence and no conclusive circumstantial evidence that proves abduction by extraterrestrial biological entities. Given the caveat that this investigation remains incomplete, there is also no conclusive evidence that Haley has been monitored or harassed by military operatives.

Government Response

Just as with the Roswell incident, government officials say Haley's story about a spaceship crash is false. They insist they know nothing at all about alien beings. However, the government did investigate the issue during the early years of the UFO phenomenon.

In 1948, soon after the first modern UFO sighting, it created a UFO research study named Project Sign, later renamed Project Blue Book. This project recommended that the U.S. military control all information and research on UFOs. Ufologists credit Project Blue Book with all of the government secrecy surrounding UFOs.

Partially because of this secrecy, the U.S. Central Intelligence Agency (CIA) decided to investigate the phenomenon itself and in 1953 established the Robertson Panel. The scientists on the panel took just twelve hours to conclude that no one had seen any alien spaceships and suggested that the air force work harder to dismiss these sightings and end "UFO hysteria."

"In the fall of 1992, [Leah] Haley . . . completed a Fantasy Prone Test given to numerous abductees by the Center for UFO Studies (CUFOS). According to [ufologist John] Carpenter: 'It revealed that she was less likely than the normal person to be fantasy prone. She fell in the frank, down-to-earth, conservative range.'"

A. J. S. Rayl, in *Omni* magazine

"Theoretically, Haley could be experiencing an altered state of consciousness—caused by anything from a food allergy to a physical problem in the brain—and having these fantastic experiences in which she has seemingly real feelings and images associated with being abducted by aliens, and which can even include physical manifestations."

Psychologist Keith Harary, in *Omni* magazine

A 1960 photo of the staff of Project Blue Book, a committee established by the government to investigate reports of UFOs. The project's last director, Hector Quintanilla, is shown seated.

Meanwhile, people continued to report UFOs. In March 1966, eighty-six college students in Michigan saw one hovering over a field. Later at another site in Michigan, several individuals reported seeing a large, red object flying near a marsh. The air force reluctantly sent a Project Blue Book investigator, J. Allen Hynek, to study both incidents. Hynek decided that the witnesses had actually seen swamp gas caused by the release of methane gas from rotting vegetation.

The press called Hynek's explanation a farce. According to Jacobs in his book *Secret Life*:

> Hynek's investigation had produced exactly the opposite effect the Air Force had intended. Instead of quieting the public's interest in UFOs, the swamp gas explanation seemed to give credence to the people who were charging that the Air Force was engaged in a cover-up.

Then-congressman Gerald Ford called for a congressional investigation into the matter. In April 1966 a House committee told the air force to study the UFO phenomenon more seriously. Subsequently, the air force awarded a $572,146 contract to the University of Colorado for the study of UFOs.

The Condon Report

The University of Colorado created a committee to study the files of Project Blue Book. This committee was led by physicist Edward U. Condon, whose attitude towards UFOs was biased from the beginning. He told many people he thought the issue was nonsense.

An artist's depiction of the strange glowing phenomenon that can be caused by swamp gas.

Condon's staff seemed to hold a similar opinion. In an August 1966 memorandum, project coordinator Robert Low told committee members how they should promote their upcoming UFO study. His memo stated:

> The trick would be to describe the project so that, to the public, it would appear a totally objective study but, to the scientific community, would present the image of a group of nonbelievers trying their best to be objective but having an almost zero expectation of finding a [flying] saucer.

Not surprisingly, when the Condon Committee issued its final report in 1968, it said that the UFO phenomenon did not deserve further study. Condon said that his staff had found "no direct evidence whatever of a convincing nature . . . for the claim that any UFOs represent spacecraft visiting Earth from another civilization."

The End of Scientific Study

Because of the Condon Report, the air force ended Project Blue Book, and public skepticism grew. At a UFO symposium in December 1969, sponsored by the American Institute of Aeronautics and Astronautics (AIAA), most speakers supported the position that UFOs were not extraterrestrial in nature. The government had effectively discouraged alternative points of view within the scientific community.

As a result, many scientists stopped investigating UFOs. Psychologists began to study abductees' stories instead. Their research made people wonder whether abductees were somehow causing the abduction experience themselves.

Physicist Edward U. Condon led a committee sponsored by the U.S. government to investigate UFO claims. The Condon Report, put out by his committee, concluded that due to lack of evidence the UFO phenomenon did not deserve further study.

Five

Are Abductions Purely Psychological?

Skeptics believe that alien abductions occur only within the human mind. They say abductees are causing their experience themselves, through imagination or other mental processes. Surprisingly, some ufologists think this as well. They argue openly with associates who insist the aliens must be coming from a distant planet.

The community of ufologists has been split into two groups because of this issue. Are the aliens real creatures from across the galaxy? Or are they products of the human mind?

Hallucinations and Fantasies

Such disagreements delight skeptics. They say ufologists cannot agree because they just do not understand the abduction phenomenon. Skeptics remain convinced that abduction experiences are always the result of mental instability, hallucination, or fantasy.

Philip Klass believes that abductees need psychiatric help. In addition, he thinks that abductees as a group are more likely to have fantasies than other people. In his book *UFO Abductions*, Klass quotes the research of psychologists Dr. Sheryl C. Wilson and Dr. T. X. Barber:

There exists a small group of individuals (possibly four percent of the population) who fantasize a large part of the time, who typically "see," "hear," "smell," and "touch" and fully experience what they fantasize; and who can be labeled fantasy-prone individuals.

Klass labels all abductees "fantasy-prone individuals."

David Jacobs disagrees with this diagnosis. In his book *Secret Life*, he says:

The abduction phenomenon has no strong element of personal fantasy. . . . Most abductees' lives contain nothing that would have such a strong effect upon them that they would hallucinate a full-scale, copiously detailed abduction event that they desperately do not want to have.

Klass counters that abductees *do* want to have these experiences. He reasons: "Instead of feeling guilty for being a day-dreamer, a fantasy-prone person who tells a tale of UFO-abduction . . . can quickly become a celebrity by appearing on radio and television talk-shows."

Encounter-Prone Personalities

Psychiatrist Kenneth Ring agrees with Klass that abductees do share certain psychological similarities. However, like Jacobs, he rejects the idea that abductees have fantasy-prone personalities. Instead, he argues that they have *encounter*-prone personalities. In other words, abductees are not more likely to fantasize than anyone else. They are just more likely to encounter something strange.

Ring explains that abductees have many traits in common with people who share mystical or visionary experiences. They accept the possibility that the world is not always as it seems, they are interested in alternative explanations for reality, and they know that unusual things can happen.

Psychiatrist Kenneth Ring believes that abductees have encounter-prone personalities, making them more likely than most people to encounter something unusual.

In many instances, these people have suffered childhood trauma or abuse. Ring theorizes that this abuse caused them to develop "an extended range of human perception beyond normally recognized limits." In other words, a person who is suffering great pain must use all of his or her mental power to endure it. Perhaps this mental effort heightens the senses. Could it be that abuse victims are able to see and hear things that others cannot see or hear?

Childhood Abuse

Other researchers think the idea of heightened senses is nonsense. However, they do agree that childhood abuse is closely related to alien abduction experiences, and some believe that memories of childhood abuse are the source of the entire abduction experience.

Many studies suggest that childhood suffering is not always remembered the way it really happened. Instead the mind recalls the trauma in a distorted way. In abduction stories, this might mean that the aliens represent human beings who hurt the abductees years ago. Jacobs explains: "[This] theory postulates that the victims are so traumatized by abuse they suffered as children that they forced the incidents out of their conscious memory; now, years later, the painful memories have resurfaced in disguised form."

Perhaps as adults, abductees have simply transformed their memories of childhood abuse into abduction scenarios. Just as they were once helpless children in the hands of capricious, violent adults, now they are helpless adults in the hands of cold, uncaring aliens.

This child-abuse theory is accepted by many psychologists and skeptics. However, Jacobs believes it is a false theory. He argues that many abduction memories relate to adult rather than childhood events. He also accurately points out that

According to the birth-trauma theory, abductees are transforming the memory of their birth into abduction memories. The dark tunnel of the alien spaceship is the memory of the dark tunnel of the birth canal, and the bright examining room is really the hospital delivery room.

not all abductees have been abused. Many of them have no history of childhood trauma.

Birth Trauma

But some researchers say that *all* people have suffered a childhood trauma, that simply being born is a painful event. These researchers think that abductees are people remembering their own births.

Professor Alvin Lawson says that every human being carries a memory of birth because the process was so traumatic. However, this memory is so deep and difficult to access that most people cannot recall it at all. A few people, however, remember it symbolically, and Lawson believes that abductees have simply transformed their birth memory into an abduction memory.

This birth-trauma theory suggests that the dark tunnel of the alien spaceship might really be the dark tunnel of the birth canal. At the end of the tunnel, the aliens' brightly lit examining room might be the hospital room where babies are delivered. And the strange, mouthless aliens might symbolize human doctors wearing medical masks.

Debunking the Birth-Trauma Theory

But David Jacobs criticizes such comparisons. He says that Professor Lawson is wrong to equate "the profound mental effects of being born . . . to abductee stories of going through a dark passage and then seeing little fetuslike people with large heads in bright rooms while lying on a table."

Jacobs argues that all births are different. For instance, babies delivered by cesarean section do not travel down a dark passage. Jacobs says:

> The minds of newborn abductees would have to contain countless bits of specific identical information relating to their birth environment, regardless of whether their eyes were closed, whether they were born in a dark area, whether other people were present, and so forth. Presumably, all babies would retain the endless details of many other "traumatic" events as well.

Jacobs believes that if people were able to remember their own births, even symbolically, they would also be able to remember other painful infant events. How many people recall their first vaccinations?

Some people who support the birth-trauma theory think that we combine these memories of early medical procedures with the ones related to birth. In trying to remember the time when we were confused, helpless babies, we transform human doctors into aliens. Abduction stories therefore result from an infant's view of all medical examinations.

But Jacobs does not believe that the birth-trauma theory adequately explains why abductees say aliens look the way they do. Abductee descriptions are very specific, rich in detail, and surprisingly consis-

"Somehow I find it hard to believe that the major governments of the world have been spending much time, energy, and money to investigate mental projections from our theorized collective unconscious."

Raymond Fowler, *The Watchers*

"There's an internal reality that everyone shares. . . . The scary thing is, we all have the same details in our nervous system [to enable us to create abduction imagery]; anybody can become an abductee."

Ronald K. Siegel, associate research professor of psychiatry at UCLA, in *Omni* magazine

tent. Jacobs argues that this means the aliens cannot be some kind of symbolic memory of a human medical event. Therefore, they must be real.

The Imaginal Realm

But psychiatrist Kenneth Ring argues that the word *real* needs redefining. He thinks that aliens do exist, but in a reality other than our own. Ring has decided that the abduction experience is one of several "mystical and visionary states" within the human mind. People who exist in one of these alternate states are connected to another reality.

Ring calls this reality the imaginal realm. The imaginal realm is another world, "the cumulative product of imaginative thought itself," and exists as an actual place. In his book *The Omega Project*, Ring quotes French Islamic scholar Henry Corbin:

> It must be understood that the [imaginal] world . . . is perfectly real. Its reality is more irrefutable and more coherent than that of the empirical world where reality is perceived by the senses. Upon returning, the beholders of this world are perfectly aware of having been "elsewhere." . . . For this reason we definitely cannot qualify it as being imaginary in the current sense of the word, i.e., unreal or nonexistent. [The imaginal] world . . . is ontologically as real as the world of the senses and that of the intellect. . . . We must be careful not to confuse it with the imagination identified by so-called modern man with "fantasy."

Ring explains that people in the imaginal realm have "imaginal bodies" and seem as solid as we are. Up until now, however, most of us have been unable to see them. Ring thinks abductees are people who have suddenly found themselves able to see creatures from the imaginal realm. They have learned how to bridge the gap between the two realities.

Ring believes that the human mind is evolving to allow this to happen and that eventually more and more people will someday be able to contact creatures from the imaginal realm. Ring says the abduction phenomenon means "that we could be in the beginning stages of a major shift in levels of consciousness that will eventually lead to humanity's being able to live in two worlds at once—the physical and the imaginal."

Interestingly, Ring developed his theories about the abduction experience and the imaginal realm while investigating near-death experiences. A near-death experience is reported when doctors are able to revive someone whose heart has stopped beating. Upon awakening, these near-death experiencers (NDErs) sometimes tell stories that Ring finds strikingly similar to abduction memories.

The Near-Death Experience Tunnel

Just as abductees talk about walking or floating down a spaceship tunnel to a brightly lit examining room, NDErs say they floated out of their bodies and traveled down a long tunnel with a bright light at the end of it. For example, one NDEr told Ring:

> I floated for a while and then was drawn down a long dark passageway with a very clear bright white light at the end. Soon I was enveloped and felt reunited with many familiar but undefinable entities. I felt a total knowing, an absence of conflict, complete peace.

Ring believes that during their near-death experiences, NDErs have entered the same imaginal realm as abductees. He says some of them have also seen the abductees' "aliens." He tells of one NDEr who said:

> There was a light toward the end of the tunnel but before I could reach it, two figures appeared outlined in light. They communicated with me through my mind, telepathically. I recognized one of the figures as being my father. He confirmed and agreed with everything conveyed by his companion who seemed to have great authority, like an angel or one of God's helpers.

An artist's depiction of the long tunnel often seen by abductees and by those who have had near-death experiences. Are abductees and NDErs experiencing the same imaginal realm?

Ring compares the telepathic powers of the angels to those of abductees' aliens.

Ring believes that even though abductees and NDErs reach the imaginal realm through different means, they share the same altered mental state while there. Abductees begin to see creatures from the imaginal realm on their own. NDErs can only do so after the death process has forced them into a new reality.

Ring says that abductees and NDErs have another important thing in common. They both leave the imaginal realm with a feeling that the earth's environment is in trouble. Abductees often report that the aliens showed them pictures of earth being destroyed in an environmental disaster. Similarly, during near-death experiences many NDErs see "a terrifying vision of global cataclysm." As a result, abductees and NDErs both come away from their experiences with a greater concern for the environment.

Spirituality

Abductees and NDErs also both leave the imaginal realm with a heightened sense of spirituality. Ring's studies reveal that after their experience, both groups become "more altruistic, have greater social concern and spirituality," and show an "appreciation for life, [an increase in] self-acceptance, concern for others, [a decrease] in materialism, and a quest for meaning and spirituality."

However, Ring adds that this does *not* mean these people become more involved with a particular religion. In fact, a majority of them abandon organized religions to follow a more universal doctrine of beliefs. One abductee explains that she rejected organized religions because of "their prejudice of each other."

Ring expected to find that NDErs come away from their experiences with heightened spirituality. After all, they have been brought back to life from the dead. However, he was surprised to find that people abducted by aliens say their experiences made them more spiritual, too.

Ring eventually traced abductees' spirituality to a belief that the aliens were sent to earth to help rather than harm humans. Most of the abductees Ring interviewed said: "There are higher order intelligences that have a concern with the welfare of our planet." Some of these people felt the aliens were sent to earth by God.

Magic and Ritual

Ring believes that spirituality is a key component of the imaginal realm. He points out that

"When in 1987 folklorist Dr. Ed Bullard analyzed 270 abduction cases from all over the world, he found such a consistency among the reports, from the look of the aliens to the idiosyncrasies of their demands, that he concluded that they could not have had a common source (as a folk story would). . . . Essentially the same thing seemed to be happening to people of entirely different occupations, background, and nationalities."

Peter Brookesmith, *UFO: The Complete Sightings*

"Could the meetings with UFO entities be . . . artificial constructions? Consider their changing character. In the United States, they appear as science fiction monsters. In South America, they are sanguinary and quick to get into a fight. In France, they behave like rational, Cartesian, peace-loving tourists. . . . The entire mystery we are discussing contains all the elements of a myth that could be utilized to serve political or sociological purposes."

Jacques Vallee, *Passport to Magonia*

modern people have lost touch with mythology and magic. Perhaps the abduction experience is a way for people to return to their spiritual roots. Ring says the phenomenon "may presage the shamanizing of modern humanity."

Ring is suggesting that abductees might be modern-day shamans. Shamans are people who believe that magic is an important part of life. They perform rituals to guide believers from the visible world to an invisible spiritual world.

Many tribal cultures have ancient rituals that require an individual to leave the group and undergo some kind of trial. Ring says that stories about abduction and near-death experiences remind him of these rituals. In both cases, a person travels to an otherworldly place and returns with a new outlook on life.

Ring believes that the abduction phenomenon fulfills the same purpose. It encourages human beings to evolve to a higher level of consciousness. Abductees see creatures that no one else sees. Therefore Ring thinks abductees are experiencing the next stage of human evolution.

Abductee Whitley Strieber also connects the abduction phenomenon to human evolution. In the foreword to Ring's book, Strieber writes:

> It may be that the direction of evolution is toward immortality and away from the physical, that from the very first something has been seeking to escape the physical world. It escaped the bottom of the sea and went flying in the water, then it escaped the water itself, then it took flight above the land, and now it seeks finally to escape the physical altogether—which is the message behind all religion, behind all unexplained experience, behind all culture.

Bizarre Theory

David Jacobs rejects this idea completely. He does not believe that human evolution has anything

"IF THAT ISN'T MY IMAGINATION, I'D BE
SCARED STIFF!"

to do with alien abduction. He says abductees are neither connected to some kind of alternate reality nor seeing creatures who come from an imaginal realm.

He calls attention to Ring's statement that the imaginal realm is "the cumulative product of imaginative thought itself." Jacobs interprets this to mean that people's imaginations have actually created the imaginal realm and all the creatures who inhabit it. Jacobs does not believe that the human mind can create real, solid aliens. But even if it could, he argues, why would anyone want to create aliens? In his book *Secret Life*, Jacobs states:

> [The imaginal-realm] theory substitutes one bizarre series of events for another. If it was [sic] possible, then human beings would be creating many alternative realities and would have been doing so for all time. But the creation of an alternative reality that would terrorize its creator, cause her to experience physical damage, and then make her live in fear that it will happen again seems unreasonable when people might instead create physical realities wherein their deepest pleasurable fantasies could be played out. No evidence whatsoever has been presented to suggest that this theory has any viability.

Dreams Made Real

Jacobs says no one would choose to create an unpleasant, abducting alien. Physicist Thomas A. Bearden suggests abductees could be creating aliens by accident. He says UFOs might result from the release of energy that takes place during a mental process like dreaming. Peter Brookesmith, in his book *UFO: The Complete Sightings*, explains Bearden's thesis:

> Bearden suggests that mental images have a physical reality that is "at right angles" to the observable physical world—much as magnetism works "at right angles" to electricity, but remains inseparable from it. But the two realities can interfere with each other. Bearden believes that the purpose of dreams is to deal with emotional conflicts, but in so doing they also put stress on those conflicts; the resultant tension creates an interference with the material world and finds release in the creation of "tulpoid" forms— material entities of psychic origin, which observers interpret as UFOs.

Bearden uses his theory only to explain UFOs. However, a few people have applied Bearden's ideas to alien abductions and suggest that alien beings could be human nightmares made real.

The Collective Unconscious

Some psychiatrists agree that dreamers can create aliens. However, they say that these aliens are not real, solid creatures, nor do they exist in any imaginal realm. Abductees are simply dreaming in the most ordinary sense of the word.

Psychiatrist Carl Jung studied people's dreams and discovered that they all contain the same basic images, regardless of a person's culture. He called these common images "archetypes" and said that they symbolize humanity's deepest desires and fears.

Psychiatrist Carl Jung theorized that abduction stories are symbolic dreams stemming from deep-rooted desires and fears.

Jung theorized that all people experience the same archetypes because all people have the same ancestral memories. In other words, human genes pass on more than just hair color or eye color. They contain ancient memories, which Jung believed were stored within a part of the mind called the "collective unconscious."

Jung related the collective unconscious to the abduction phenomenon in his 1959 book *Flying Saucers: A Modern Myth*. He said that abductees might not be seeing real aliens but archetypal images. In other words, abduction stories are symbolic dreams that reflect deep-seated emotions and other communal mental experiences.

Aliens as Folklore

Jung says that images of aliens have existed since ancient times, but David Jacobs counters that alien abductions are a modern occurrence. Jacobs rejects Jung's theory because it "does not consider the puzzling fact that the abduction syndrome is a recent phenomenon confined to the twentieth century." Therefore, Jacobs argues, the collective unconscious could not be an ancient memory stored within a person's genes. He concludes: "[The theory] would have to prove that the collective unconscious is dynamic and can come into being and change around the world at any given time regardless of culture."

Many researchers say Jacobs is wrong—that alien abductions were reported in ancient times. However, they were reported not as fact but as folklore. Jacques Vallee, in his book *Passport to Magonia: On UFOs, Folklore, and Parallel Worlds*, explains that abduction stories have a long history in folklore:

> The folklore of every culture . . . had a rich reservoir of stories about humanoid beings that flew in the sky, used devices that seemed in advance of the technology of the time, and said

strangely beautiful, although absurd, things to those with whom they came in contact. These beings abducted humans, and their victims uniformly reported an alteration of the sense of time when they were in the beings' company.

Vallee's research uncovered a one-hundred-year history of alien encounters. Sometimes the aliens were called fairies. Other times they were called gods. Whatever their names, in most instances these strange beings overpowered or tricked unsuspecting human beings. In another of his books, *Dimensions: A Casebook of Alien Contact*, Vallee states that the current abduction phenomenon might belong to this "age-old and worldwide myth that has shaped our belief structures, our scientific expectations, and our view of ourselves."

Given this connection between UFOs and folklore, Peter Brookesmith concludes that alien abduction is some kind of mental experience:

> My own conviction is that the human mind is inextricably involved with all UFO phenomena, from "simple" sightings of flying disks to complex, full-blown abduction accounts. I say this partly because of the astonishing variety in UFO reports, and partly because UFOs and aliens seem to single out individuals or small groups of people to whom they reveal themselves—while remaining unseen by others close by. But mainly I say it because the secret history of the UFO stretches back into antiquity. The similarities between modern UFO reports and ancient tales of fiery wheels, dragons and portents in the sky are truly remarkable; moreover, there are extraordinary parallels between today's descriptions of abductions by aliens and archaic accounts of folk being "stolen" by elves and goblins.

Aliens as Elves

Abductee Whitley Strieber argues that the historical connection between folklore and abduction

"Jungian extremists would insist that the powers of the collective mind could produce such physical effects including scars found on abductees! This, of course, cannot be demonstrated scientifically."

Raymond Fowler, *The Watchers*

"Could it be that life itself is a mechanism by which some hidden, inner reality is touching and feeling its way into the physical world? Are we a medium of exchange, a communications device, an extraordinary construction designed to bridge the gulf between the physical world and something else?"

Whitley Strieber, in *The Omega Project*

does not rule out the possibility that aliens are real. Perhaps ancient stories about elves were true—and perhaps these so-called elves were really aliens from another planet.

Strieber says that we should be trying harder to discover the identity of folklore's ancient creatures. If we knew who or what they were, we might not be as frightened by them. In his book *Transformation: The Breakthrough*, Strieber states:

> Abduction by nonhuman beings is a part of much folklore. Whether the abductors are called demons, gods, fairies, or aliens, the experience is always devastating to its victims. Because we have refused to study the subject, we remain ignorant, and the experience is as hard now as it was a thousand years ago.

Strieber believes that our fear comes from the unknown.

No Connection

But David Jacobs rejects any connection between the aliens and fairies, dwarfs, gnomes, or elves. In his book *Secret Life*, he contends:

> The adherents of this theory disconnect such folktales from their original social and cultural context and then present them as fact in a completely different milieu as if they have a life of their own. The only difference, they claim, is that abduction stories are now more technologically advanced. But they present only vague and general similarities to show that the abduction phenomenon is related to myth, legend, and folklore such as superficial stories about "changelings," little people, or gods who live in the heavens. For adherents of the folklore hypothesis, facile resemblances become complex modern duplicates.

In other words, Jacobs does not believe that aliens have much in common with elves. Alien abduction stories are not simply updated folklore about elves who have learned technology. He and others believe that the details of the abduction phenomenon are too complex to be explained this way.

Many Possibilities

Even some proponents of the alien-folklore connection admit the idea has flaws. For example, Whitley Strieber remarks that he might be wrong about the aliens being modern elves. He sees many other possibilities for their identity:

> It should not be forgotten that the visitors . . . represent the most powerful of all forces acting in human culture. They may be

Some ufologists believe that ancient stories about elves or fairies are really stories about aliens from other planets.

extraterrestrials managing the evolution of the human mind. Or they may represent the presence of mind on another level of being. Perhaps our fate is eventually to leave the physical world altogether and join them in that strange hyper-reality from which they seem to emerge.

Strieber would like to believe that aliens are a complex creation of the human mind. However, he acknowledges that they could also be real beings who come from another planet, dimension, or time. Strieber says this simpler explanation is more frightening. He confesses:

> I longed to decide that the visitors were part of my mind. As an intellectual I felt terribly threatened by the idea of extraterrestrial or "other" intelligence. I did not like it and I did not want it to be true. One of the most difficult things I've had to face is the frank prospect that it is true.

> We hide from the visitors. We hide in beliefs. They're the gods. They're gentry, dwarfs, elves. They're demons or angels. Aliens. The unconscious. The oversoul. Hallucinations. Mass hysteria. Lies. You name it. But what they never are, what we never allow ourselves to face, is the truth.

Aliens Are Real

The truth, argues ufologist Budd Hopkins, is that aliens are real. They are external beings who operate under their own set of rules. They do not fit human ideas of what aliens are supposed to be, and our science fiction is meaningless to them. They are not "kindly, helpful, all-powerful 'Space Brothers,'" nor are they "'Space Invaders' swooping down upon us to conquer and colonize our planet."

Hopkins finds it significant that aliens do not fit our preconceived notions about them. This means we did not create them. In his book *Missing Time*,

Hopkins says: "By any standard of comparison, the UFO phenomenon . . . seems less like a simplistic product of popular fantasy than it does a highly complex, morally ambiguous and self-contained external reality. A reality, I should add, that none of us understands."

Psychiatrist John E. Mack, in his book *Abduction: Human Encounters with Aliens*, adds that anyone who cannot believe aliens are real is "either unfamiliar with the rich complexity of the abduction phenomenon itself, or . . . wedded to a worldview in which the idea of an intelligence or beings from outside of the earth visiting us is simply not possible." In other words, ignorance and prejudice keep people from believing in aliens who come from another planet.

But if aliens are real, and if they do come from another planet, why would they be visiting earth? What could they hope to achieve by contacting us? Why do they behave in such mysterious ways? Some researchers argue that we can discover the answers to these questions by studying abduction stories more carefully.

Six

Why Would Aliens Be Visiting Earth?

Ufologists who believe in real aliens have several theories about why these extraterrestrial beings might be visiting earth. Their theories are based on the details of alien behavior as told in abduction stories.

A Research Study

Many people think that the aliens are acting like human zoologists who study wild animals. Says abductee Kathy Mitchell in her book *Abducted!*: "If you compare a UFO abduction to the capture and testing of wild animals to record their migration and living habits—sedation, capture, examination, and tagging for future identification—you will find striking similarities."

Abductee Mac McMahon agrees. He says that the aliens remind him of veterinarians. In Budd Hopkins's book *Missing Time*, McMahon states: "[Their attitude] wasn't an antihuman attitude, it was more of a 'We're going to check you out, pup. Get up there on the table' sort of deal. I get the same impression when I take a dog to the vet."

Perhaps the aliens are conducting a research study on human beings and perhaps the abductees' implants are monitoring devices. Budd Hopkins says:

One inescapable inference to be drawn from this pattern is that a very long-term, in-depth study is being made of a relatively large sample of humans, and that this study may involve mechanical implants of some sort. . . . If such a long-term monitoring system is going on, it would help explain the decades of surreptitious UFO behavior and the absence of direct communication.

However, Hopkins adds that the aliens might be doing more than merely studying human beings. Given abductee reports of ova extraction, he says:

Can an advanced technology, whose home base is outside Earth, be experimenting . . . with various human genetic combinations? Our own present-day science has successfully mated sperm and ovum in a test tube, implanted the fertilized egg in a female body, and brought the fetus to term. Cloning is a much talked about area of current experimentation, moving slowly from lower animal forms towards man himself. There is no way to estimate what a radically advanced technology might be capable of.

Alien Thieves

Budd Hopkins further suggests that the aliens might be coming to earth to steal something:

What if the UFO occupants are *taking* something from their captives? Many people assume . . . that if alien beings could travel across distances ranging upwards from four light-years (the distance of the nearest star, Alpha Centauri, from Earth) then they must indeed be supermen, and the idea is therefore ludicrous that they might need anything we possess. Even more outrageous, they add, is the idea that extraterrestrials might be afraid of us, or vulnerable in any way. But why assume any of these things? We may indeed possess something—a natural resource, an element, a genetic structure—that an alien culture might desire to use, for example, as experimental raw material.

Many abductees and ufologists support Hopkins's theory that the aliens have somehow become unable to produce their own genetic material and need ours. David Jacobs, in his book *Secret Life*, says:

> One of the purposes for which UFOs travel to Earth is to abduct humans to help aliens produce other Beings. It is not a program of reproduction, but one of *production*. They are not here to help us. They have their own agenda, and we are not allowed to know its full parameters.

But Jacques Vallee does not see why the aliens would need to keep abducting people to improve their gene pool. In his book *Revelations* he explains that human scientists, given a little genetic material, could eventually duplicate, or clone, human beings without having to kidnap so many people. He explains:

> Equipped with the state-of-the-art techniques of current U.S. medicine, it would be conceivable that the entire human race could, in time, be restarted from this pool of genetic material. Indeed gene therapy and the creation of hybrid species is well within our theoretical horizon, even if it has not completely been reduced to practice. None of these accomplishments require the procedural behavior of the "alien doctors" described by abduction researchers.

Philip Klass thinks the whole idea of alien genetic experiments is laughable. In his book *UFO Abductions*, he questions why aliens would want to "enrich their stock" with abductees who are neither top athletes nor otherwise gifted. He mentions Debbie Jordan, who has many health problems but claims that her ova have created several alien babies. Klass says:

> If [Budd] Hopkins's theory of an extraterrestrial genetic experiment is correct, then the choice of [Debbie Jordan] as a subject suggests that the objective might be to *degrade* the health of

"It is difficult to ignore the fact that the UFO abduction phenomenon is taking place [at a time when] human power and greed, made invincible by technologies that are ravaging the earth's environment, are bringing the planet's biosystems to the edge of collapse. . . . Abductions seem to be concerned primarily with . . . changing human consciousness to prevent the destruction of the earth's life, and a joining of two species for the creation of a new evolutionary form."

John Mack, *Abduction*

"The simple truth is this: if there is a form of life and consciousness that operates on properties of space-time we have not yet discovered, then it does not have to be extraterrestrial. It could come from any place and any time, even from our own environment."

Jacques Vallee, *Revelations*

Aliens take a hybrid fetus from an abductee. Many abductees contend that these hybrid children are meant to inhabit the earth after the human race has died out.

extraterrestrials, perhaps to *reduce* their lifespan to solve an overpopulation problem. But if that were their objective, it would be so much easier to abduct [Jordan] and take her back to their native planet than to have to make the long journey to Earth every time they wanted another of her ova.

Hybrid Babies

But some abductees argue that the aliens have to perform their procedures on earth. They say that the half-human, half-alien babies are the reason for this behavior. The aliens need a variety of humans to interact with these babies on a regular basis. Otherwise the children will not survive.

Many abductees think these hybrids represent alien attempts to create better human beings. In the book *Abduction*, an abductee named Peter tells psychiatrist John Mack that the aliens "want our love and how it is we love and care and have such compassion. They also are terrified of our anger and our ability to hate and kill and all that stuff, and they're trying to get the two apart." Peter says that through genetics the aliens hope to take "the higher human qualities and separate them from the lower human qualities and somehow . . . reincorporate them into our race."

Abductee Debbie Jordan also views the aliens' creation of hybrid babies in positive terms. In her book *Abducted!* she says:

> Producing a half-human-half-alien baby would appear to be a sensible step for such a scrawny-looking species as the [aliens]. Comparing our species and theirs, we appear to be far superior, physically speaking. They are no doubt eons ahead of us mentally. If we could combine the best attributes of both breeds, just imagine the possibilities of such a civilization.

Earth's New Inhabitants

Many abductees believe that these hybrid children are meant to inhabit earth after human beings are gone. Some abductees claim that the aliens have communicated this information to them through thoughts, either during the abduction experience or later when they were back at home. Budd Hopkins explains: "In some UFO abductions . . . extended telepathic conversations have taken place between the abductors and their captives. Occasional messages, and even warnings, often pertaining to our misuse of the environment, have been reported."

John Mack tells of an abductee named Scott who says a disaster will someday destroy all human life. Mack says Scott believes:

> Major changes in the world are coming. . . . The aliens will only come "when it's safer." But that will not occur until there are "less and less" of us as we die off from disease, especially more

"When you see the babies it's weird, but when you see the little fetuses, there's no doubt about what they're doing. They're breeding us."

Abductee Karen Morgan, in *Secret Life*.

"Among the list of stupid things a superior extraterrestrial civilization with any knowledge of biology would not need to do would be to scoop up skin samples and remove embryos from millions of terrified Americans. The abduction theories make for good television entertainment but for very bad science."

Jacques Vallee, *Revelations*

communicable forms of AIDS that will reach plague proportions.

Scott also believes that the atmosphere of the aliens' own planet was destroyed by something they themselves accidentally caused. Their planet's surface became unlivable, and the aliens moved underground into an "artificial environment." Mack recounts:

> With considerable resistance Scott admitted that the intention of the aliens was to "live here" (on Earth) but without us, unless "humans change," in which case "we might be able to live together." Then he contrasted the ways of humans with the aliens. Human beings "are alone" and "they don't share." In the alien realm "nobody's in their own world" and everybody knows everything. There are no secrets.

Mack acknowledges the possibility that the abductees

> may be participating in some sort of project of species merger and evolution. The purpose of this project may be to create new life-forms that are more spiritually evolved and less aggressive, while retaining the acute sensory possibilities that accompany the dense embodiment of human physical existence.

In other words, the aliens might be trying to create their idea of the "perfect" earth inhabitant. Such creatures would possess human strength, human size, and only the most positive human emotions. They would never be violent.

Earth's Gardeners

But why would the aliens want to create this kind of being? Some people have suggested that a strong but nonviolent creature would make a perfect slave. Perhaps the aliens want to use human beings as their servants. However, many abductees believe the aliens are trying to help us, not trying to exploit us.

John Mack tells of one abductee named Carlos who says the aliens want to protect earth's environment. Carlos "clearly believes that the aliens, however awkward, or even brutal, their methods, are trying to arrest our destructive behavior." Aliens must change human beings because humans are "self-destructive and therefore destructive to all sorts of things."

Carlos describes the aliens as being "like little tiny drones of a vaster complexity" who are "in the

"There they go—showing off their superiority over nature again."

service of survival." He thinks that some higher power has told the aliens to keep earth from collapsing. Carlos believes this is why the aliens are warning abductees not to destroy their environment, and perhaps why they might be creating new inhabitants for earth that are half human, half alien. Carlos says the aliens are "Earth gardeners trying really hard to instruct us to find a plenitude and not to be caught in the human impulses towards extinction." He believes the aliens want people to discover that "plenitude in the environment, a plenitude of the garden Earth."

The Watchers

Another abductee, Betty Andreasson Luca, also believes that the aliens want to save earth. In his book *The Watchers*, Raymond Fowler says an alien told Luca "that [his people] are the *caretakers* of nature and natural forms—*The Watchers*. They love mankind. They love the planet earth and they have been caring for it and man since man's beginning. . . . Man is destroying much of nature."

Luca also reported that alien abductions were "being done to monitor environmental effects on the body and to achieve restoration of the human form. Again, they stressed . . . that the balance of nature on earth was in jeopardy." In other words, Luca believes that the aliens not only want to improve the earth but also want to improve its inhabitants.

Fowler reasons that this is why the number of alien abductions has increased in recent decades. As environmental pollution and human health has grown worse, the aliens have expanded their activity. Fowler therefore concludes that "the acceleration of UFO activity is directly related to Man's increasing destruction of earth's life-supporting environment. . . . Man must engage in an immediate all-inclusive program to repair and protect the environment."

Many abductees share Fowler's opinion that human beings must act on the aliens' warnings about earth's environment. John Mack says:

> Virtually every abductee receives information about the destruction of the earth's ecosystem and feels compelled to do something about it. . . . Abductees experience powerful images of vast destruction, with the collapse of governmental and economic infrastructures and the total pollution and desertification of the planet.

A Symbolic Dream

Kenneth Ring believes that abduction experiences like Luca's support his imaginal realm theory. He thinks the aliens' environmental warnings are symbolic messages sent from human minds. Alien examinations of human beings represent our own evaluation of what we are doing wrong as a species. Ring says: "We (humanity) are being examined.

Betty Andreasson Luca, posing with reproductions of the aliens she says she encountered, believes that aliens have come to earth to save it from destruction by humans.

What is the symbolic meaning of this action? [Philosopher Michael] Grosso suggests that we are a sick species, we have gone off the mark." Ring quotes Grosso as saying:

> I cannot help thinking it is we who are in need of dire examination; it is we who have to place ourselves on an "operating table." It looks to me as if something—some intelligence—is "examining" and "operating on" us. Medical operation implies a need for healing. The latest development in UFO symbolism [i.e., the abduction narrative] contains a message about healing ourselves.

Ring asks: "What is it in ourselves that needs healing?" He finds his answer in the image of the alien, "frail and tortured-looking, his enormous black eyes reminding us, as Grosso observes, of the images we have all seen on our television screens . . . of children dying of starvation in drought-plagued Africa." The aliens represent human suffering.

Ring is suggesting that our imaginations have created the aliens to show us what might happen if we do not change our ways. These aliens have come from the imaginal realm to warn us that if pollution continues, future generations of humans will look like them. Ring says:

> The future of the human race—symbolized by the archetype of the child—is menaced as never before. We need to heal ourselves of all those tendencies—unthinking greed, mindless development, ruthless exploitation—that threaten our native habitat so severely as to make us fear that our progeny will be replicas of the stunted and deformed aliens that now infiltrate the collective nightmare that portions of humanity are dreaming.

Ring says that the hybrid babies in abduction stories prove his point that the aliens are warning us about environmental pollution. He quotes Grosso as explaining:

Taken literally, the reason [for the hybrid babies] perhaps is to revitalize *their* ailing stock. Taken symbolically, the idea of hybrids would be about *our* need to be revitalized; the need to enhance our gene pool. It certainly makes sense to say that we need to embark on evolutionary experiments, to mutate *ourselves*. In other words, if we interpret the symbolism of the abduction experience as a strange kind of species dream, the message is that our world, symbolized by the otherworld, is a dying wasteland and that we have to evolve into a higher (and hence more adaptable) species.

Psychic Telegrams

Researchers like Ring and Grosso think that human minds are the source of the aliens' environmental warnings. George C. Andrews, however, does not think our minds have *created* the aliens. Instead he thinks our minds have *called* them.

In his book *Extra-Terrestrials Among Us*, Andrews suggests that human beings have been mentally broadcasting their concerns about the environment throughout the universe. He speaks of "psychic telegrams" sent to "telepathic" aliens out in space—"a telepathic S.O.S. Mayday call for help to save the planet's biosphere." He speculates that some ancient power within the earth itself might even be sending "distress signals through space." Has earth called the aliens here to stop human destruction? Andrews says:

Some researchers theorize that the earth has sent out distress signals to aliens asking for their help in stopping human destruction.

> Are those distress signals what the UFOs have come in response to? Has Mother Earth asked to have her face cleaned? Have we been transforming our planet into a cancer cell in the body of the galaxy instead of making it the garden of the universe? Perhaps the Christian, Islamic, Hebrew, Mazdean and Hopi traditions of Judgment Day refer to the day when the Earth is once more "relieved of its heavy load."

Many other researchers have found a religious aspect to the abduction phenomenon. In his article "UFO Contactees—Heralds of the New Age" in *Unsolved UFO Sighting*s magazine, Brad Steiger says:

> In my opinion, the UFO contactees, with their emphasis upon spiritual teachings being transmitted to Earth by Space Beings, are seeking to bring "God" physically to this planet. These UFO prophets have created a blend of science and religion that offers a space-age theology that seems more applicable to a good many modern men and women.

Science and Religion

Steiger is suggesting that the aliens represent both modern science and ancient religion. He is convinced that this combination is important to today's society. In recent times, many people have rejected religion because they feel it conflicts with science. They embrace technology but stop believing in God. As a result, they feel that human beings are alone in the universe.

Steiger points out that the existence of aliens would change that feeling. If abductees are right, then human beings must consider themselves part of a greater purpose. God might not have a plan for them, but the aliens do. Steiger says we need this outlook on life. He reasons:

> In our day of fear and dread, in our time of endless chaos, pollution, fallout, rips in the ozone layer and threats of nuclear annihilation, we need a sense of meaning and purpose for existence as never before in our history as a species. If, as contact with extraterrestrial intelligences would seem to suggest, we are not alone in the universe, then life does have a meaning, for we now have the opportunity to become part of a larger community of intelligences. We may now become evolving members in a hierarchy of cosmic citizenship.

To Steiger, it does not matter whether the aliens are real or not. It does not matter where they come from. Regardless of their origin or identity, their words and purpose are the same. He says:

Whoever or whatever the Space Beings may be—whether cosmic missionaries or projections of the Higher Self—the channeled [i.e., telepathically transmitted] messages which they share may be the scriptures and theological treatises of the New Age.

Steiger is proposing that the aliens' messages are the doctrine of a new religion. This doctrine tells human beings how to live—just as the doctrines of traditional religions do. For this reason, Dr. Gordon Melton, director of the Institute of the Study of American Religion, compares abductees to religious disciples. Steiger quotes Melton as saying that UFO contactees represent "an emerging religious movement with an impetus and a life of their own."

Guardian Angels of the Earth

Steiger adds that the aliens' religious doctrine goes beyond environmental issues. Both abductees and people who say they have received alien messages from afar claim these creatures want to change our entire way of life. Steiger says:

Contactees have been told that the Space Beings hope to guide Earth to a period of great unification, when all races will shun discriminatory separations and all of humankind will recognize its responsibility to every other life form existing on the planet. The Space Beings also seek to bring about a single, solidified government, which will conduct itself on spiritual principles and permit all of its citizens to grow constructively in love.

According to Steiger, it is this emphasis on love and racial harmony that has led some people to equate the aliens with guardian angels. Such comparisons convince him that religion has to be an im-

"In focusing on the gynecological and reproductive procedures that have been performed on abductees, I have come to firmly believe there is some type of ongoing genetic manipulation that is occurring with various family generations."

Dr. Richard Neal, an obstetrician-gynecologist, in *The Watchers*

"I have come to support less and less the idea that UFOs are 'nuts and bolts' spacecraft from other worlds. . . . To me, it seems ridiculous that super intelligence would travel great distances to do relatively stupid things like stop cars, collect soil samples, and frighten people. I think we must begin to re-examine the evidence. We must begin to look closer to home."

J. Allen Hynek, in *Revelations*

portant part of UFO study. Ufologists cannot ignore the religious significance of the abduction experience. Steiger says:

> However one deals with the Flying Saucer Movement in one's own reality, the undeniable fact remains that thousands of men and women throughout the world have made the UFO a symbol of religious awakening and spiritual transformation. Some envision the UFO as their deliverer from a world fouled by its own inhabitants.

Steiger concludes that the explanation for the aliens is not as important as the experience of the aliens. We should not be spending our time arguing about the aliens themselves. Instead we should be

An artist's conception of a man defending himself against aliens. Whether alien abductions are real or in the imagination, many ufologists believe that humans should listen to the messages delivered by the abductees.

listening to what abductees are saying about their messages.

John Mack shares a similar view. He accepts that we may never know where aliens come from or what they really are. However, he believes that even if aliens remain a mystery, abduction stories can still teach us a great deal: they urge us to avoid an environmental tragedy, they warn people to change their way of life, and they offer new visions of the future. Certainly these messages deserve consideration. Mack says:

> The alien beings have come to the abductees from a source that remains unknown to us. We still do not fully grasp their purposes or their methods. . . . Some have speculated that the alien beings have mastered time travel and come to us from the future. Sometimes they even communicate that this might be so. We do not know. But the guiding or regenerative myth of the abduction phenomenon offers a new story for a world that has survived many holocausts and may yet be deterred from a final cataclysm. The abduction phenomenon, it seems clear, is about what is *yet* to come. It presents, quite literally, visions of alternative futures, but it leaves the choice to us.

"I like to believe these alien entities are doing this for the good of mankind."

Kathy Mitchell, *Abducted!*

"Contact between the races is not taking place in a scenario that has been commonly envisioned by scientists and science fiction writers: two independent worlds making careful overtures for equal and mutual benefit. Rather, it is completely one-sided. Instead of equal benefit, we see a disturbing program of apparent exploitation of one species by another."

David Jacobs, *Secret Life*

Epilogue

Choosing What to Believe

It is not surprising that skeptics and ufologists cannot agree on whether alien abductions really happen. Even abduction researchers argue among themselves about the source and meaning of abduction stories. Each researcher believes there is one right answer to the question: What exactly have abductees experienced?

Given such passionate debate and the lack of indisputable proof, ordinary people often do not know what to think. Should they listen to skeptics who insist that the whole issue is a hoax? Should they accept the existence of aliens on faith, the way someone might accept the existence of guardian angels? If faith is not enough, then how will we learn the truth?

Investigating Alien "Crime Scenes"

UFO researcher Victoria Alexander thinks she knows a way. She believes we should start treating abduction sites like crime scenes. In the article "UFO Crime Lab" by Patrick Huyghe in *Omni* magazine, Alexander explains: "After all, crimes are supposedly being committed. The aliens are accused of unlawful entries, kidnappings, assaults. . . . I think it's time we start looking at the

(Opposite page) A 1981 photo captures the image of a UFO flying over a mountain in British Columbia, Canada. Until there is proof that aliens exist, or that they do not, alien abductions will continue to be the subject of much debate.

Many skeptics like Philip Klass continue to dismiss the notion of alien abductions as nonsense, though to many they will remain a mystery.

typical bedroom abduction as a police crime-scene unit would."

Alexander is developing a kit that abduction researchers could use to investigate an alien "crime scene." She says:

> Since the vast majority of abductees claim the aliens are humanoid, not robots, there should be biological and chemical traces of their presence. If these are real events, if the aliens are real, if contact is taking place, there has to be real evidence for it—latent fingerprints, fungi, particles, whatever. It's a basic tenet of criminalistics that when any two items come in contact there will be an exchange of microscopic particles.

Alexander is excited about her idea. Skeptic Philip Klass, however, is not. He says: "In my opinion, if abductions were fact and not fantasy, we would have had impressive evidence a long, long time ago."

Unless they see an alien fingerprint and accompanying snapshot, skeptics like Klass will continue to dismiss the whole subject of ufology as nonsense. At the same time, ufologists will remain divided about the true meaning of abduction stories. Someday we might learn without doubt who is right. Until then, we are left with few clues from which to draw a conclusion. Alien abductions are still a mystery.

Organizations to Contact

**The Committee for the Scientific Investigation
of Claims of the Paranormal**
3965 Rensch Rd.
Amherst, NY 14228-2713
(716) 636-1425

This organization publishes the magazine *The
Skeptical Inquirer*. It also holds conferences and
symposiums not only on UFOs but also on a wide
variety of controversial issues. Its board members
include skeptic Philip Klass and psychologist
Elizabeth Loftus, as well as prominent psychiatrists,
physicists, astronomers, chemists, and other scientists. Its literature promotes "the need to question
everything" and says that "the real world is far more
exciting than anything the wishful thinkers can
come up with."

Mutual UFO Network (MUFON)
103 Oldtowne Rd.
Sequin, TX 78115
(210) 379-9216

This organization has been called one of the most
influential UFO groups in the United States. It publishes the *MUFON UFO Journal*, a widely read
UFO newsletter. MUFON's purpose is to gather and
disseminate information about UFOs. It documents
and studies cases of UFO sightings and alien
encounters throughout the world. It also holds conferences and symposiums on UFO-related issues,

including alien abduction. Many of the speakers at these conferences are well-known ufologists and abductees. MUFON's members include ufologists, academics, and psychologists, as well as ordinary citizens interested in UFOs.

The Program for Extraordinary Experience Research (PEER)
PO Box 382427
Cambridge, MA 02238-2427
(617) 497-5781

This organization was founded in 1993 by Harvard psychiatrist John E. Mack. It is a nonprofit research and education group that considers a variety of "extraordinary experiences." Currently, PEER is involved in a research program on alien abduction. It is soliciting abduction stories and working with therapists who are interested in this issue.

The Skeptics Society
2761 N. Marengo Ave.
Altadena, CA 91001
(818) 794-3119

This organization investigates unusual claims on a wide variety of issues to determine whether these claims "hold up to scientific scrutiny." It publishes *Skeptic* magazine and also sponsors a lecture series at Caltech University in California. Its board members include well-known magicians James Randi and Mark Edward, comedian Steve Allen, and therapist/radio–talk show host Laura Schlessinger, as well as several prominent academics and scientists. In its literature, the society quotes the philosophy of the seventeenth-century Dutch philosopher Baruch Spinoza: "I have made a ceaseless effort not to ridicule, not to bewail, not to scorn human actions, but to understand them."

For Further Exploration

Michael Arvey, *UFOs: Opposing Viewpoints*. San Diego, CA: Greenhaven Press, 1989.

Howard Blum, *Out There: The Government's Secret Quest for Extraterrestrials*. New York: Simon & Schuster, 1990.

Jerome Clark and Marcello Truzzi, *UFO Encounters: Sightings, Visitations, and Investigations*. Lincolnwood, IL: Publications International, 1992.

George M. Eberhart, *The Roswell Report: An Historical Perspective*. Chicago: J. Allen Hynek Center for UFO Studies, 1991.

Timothy Good, *Above Top Secret: The Worldwide UFO Cover-Up*. New York: William Morrow, 1988.

David M. Jacobs, *The UFO Controversy in America*. Bloomington: Indiana University Press, 1975.

Philip Klass, *UFOs: The Public Deceived*. Buffalo, NY: Prometheus Books, 1983.

George Terence Meaden, *The Circles Effect and Its Mysteries*. London: Artetech, 1990.

James E. Oberg, *UFOs and Outer Space Mysteries: A Sympathetic Skeptic's Report*. Norfolk, VA: Donning, 1982.

Terry O'Neill and Stacey L. Tipp, eds., "Are UFOs Real?" *Paranormal Phenomena: Opposing Viewpoints*. San Diego, CA: Greenhaven Press, 1991.

Jenny Randles, *UFOs and How to See Them*. New York: Sterling, 1992.

John Spencer, *World Atlas of UFOs: Sightings, Abductions, and Close Encounters*. New York: Smithmark, 1991.

Dennis Stacy, "The *Omni* Open Book Field Investigators Guide: Part One—A Guide for the Serious UFO Investigator," *Omni*, March 1995.

————,"The *Omni* Open Book Field Investigators Guide: Part Two," *Omni*, April 1995.

Walter N. Webb, *Encounter at Bluff Ledge: A UFO Case History*. Chicago: J. Allen Hynek Center for UFO Studies, 1994.

Works Consulted

Colin Andrews, "Full Circle," *International UFO Library*, vol. 3, no. 2, 1995.

George C. Andrews, *Extra-Terrestrials Among Us*. St. Paul, MN: Llewellyn Publications, 1986.

Peter Brookesmith, *UFO: The Complete Sightings*. New York: Barnes & Noble Books, 1995.

Bufo Calvin, "Extraterrestrials or Visitors Through Time?" *Strange*, no. 14, 1995.

Ed Conroy, *Report on Communion*. New York: William Morrow, 1989.

Raymond E. Fowler, *The Watchers: The Secret Design Behind UFO Abduction*. New York: Bantam, 1990.

John G. Fuller, *The Interrupted Journey: Two Lost Hours "Aboard a Flying Saucer."* New York: Dial Press, 1966.

Sonny Gordon, "Roswell," *International UFO Library*, vol. 3, no. 2, 1995.

Budd Hopkins, *Intruders: The Incredible Visitations at Copley Woods*. New York: Ballantine Books, 1987.

———, *Missing Time*. New York: Ballantine Books, 1981.

Patrick Huyghe, "Alien Implant or—Human Underwear," *Omni*, April 1995.

———, "UFO Crime Lab," *Omni*, April 1995.

David M. Jacobs, *Secret Life: Firsthand Documented Accounts of UFO Abductions*. New York: Simon & Schuster, 1992.

Debbie Jordan and Kathy Mitchell, *Abducted!* New York: Carroll & Graf, 1994.

Carl Jung, *Flying Saucers: A Modern Myth*. New York: Harcourt, Brace, 1959.

Philip Klass, *UFO Abductions*. Buffalo, NY: Prometheus Books, 1989.

Elizabeth Loftus and Katherine Ketcham, *The Myth of Repressed Memory*. New York: St. Martin's Press, 1994.

John E. Mack, *Abduction: Human Encounters with Aliens*. New York: Ballantine Books, 1994.

Donald H. Menzel and Ernest H. Taves, *The UFO Enigma: The Definitive Explanation of the UFO Phenomenon*. New York: Doubleday, 1977.

Kevin D. Randle and Donald R. Schmitt, *UFO Crash at Roswell*. New York: Avon Books, 1991.

A. J. S. Rayl, "Anatomy of an Abduction," *Omni*, February 1995.

Kenneth Ring, *The Omega Project: Near-Death Experiences, UFO Encounters, and Mind at Large*. New York: William Morrow, 1992.

Carl Sagan and Thornton Page, eds., *UFO's—A Scientific Debate*. Ithaca, NY: Cornell University Press, 1972.

Brad Steiger, "UFO Contactees—Heralds of the New Age," *Unsolved UFO Sightings*, Winter 1995.

Whitley Strieber, *Communion: A True Story*. New York: Avon Books, 1987.

———, *Transformation: The Breakthrough*. New York: Beech Tree Books/William Morrow, 1988.

Jacques Vallee, *Dimensions: A Casebook of Alien Contact*. New York: Ballantine Books, 1988.

———, *Passport to Magonia: On UFOs, Folklore, and Parallel Worlds*. Chicago: Contemporary Books, 1993.

———, *Revelations: Alien Contact and Human Deception*. New York: Ballantine Books, 1991.

Ed Walters and Frances Walters, *UFO Abductions in Gulf Breeze*. New York: Avon Books, 1994.

Index

About the Author

Patricia D. Netzley received a bachelor's degree in English from the University of California at Los Angeles (UCLA). After graduation she worked as an editor at the UCLA Medical Center, where she produced hundreds of medical articles, speeches, and pamphlets.

Netzley became a freelance writer in 1986. She is the author of three other nonfiction books for young people, *The Assassination of President John F. Kennedy* (Macmillan/New Discovery Books, 1994), *The Importance of Queen Victoria* (Lucent Books, 1996), and *The Mysterious Death of Butch Cassidy* (Lucent Books, 1997).

Netzley and her husband Raymond live in Southern California with their three children, Matthew, Sarah, and Jacob. The family has traveled a great deal and recently returned from a year in Bellingham, Washington.

Picture Credits